Messages from the Sea

Messages from the Sea

Letters and Notes from a Lost Era Found in Bottles and on Beaches Around the World

Compiled by Paul Brown

superelastic

Published in the UK by Superelastic

ISBN 978-0-9955412-1-4

www.superelasticbooks.com

Cover illustration by Franzi @ franzidraws.com

Sea life illustrations adapted from sketches by Frederick Whymper from *The Sea: Its Stirring Story* Vols 1-4, 1877-1880

www.messagesfromthesea.com

MESSAGES FROM THE SEA.

Yesterday Mr George Stamp, picked upon the beach at Sandsend, near Whitby, the following message, which had evidently been washed up by the sea:—"Boat and four hands. s.s. Rechta, floated two days; can't float much longer.—L. Good-bye." The message does not bear the appearance of being a hoax.

MESSAGES FROM THE SEA.

A soda water bottle containing the following messages written on scraps of an envelope has been picked up off Howth. near Dublin. "July 21st, 1886, Britannia, Liverpool, Captain Dawson, sinking fast, heavy sea from Rio Janeiro, passenger lost, pray for us, lifeboat No. 2." "Left June 28, frightful weather, sinking."

MESSAGE FROM THE SEA.

"GOD HELP US."

A Deal telegram says that a bottle washed ashore there contained the following message:—"God help us, we are slowly sinking. Island King."

MESSAGE FROM THE SEA.

A bottle has been found on the sands near Fleetwood, containing a piece of paper on which is written the following message:— "Brig Louisa went down yesterday. Only survivors two men out in an open boat somewhere off the coast of Ireland. Help us, for God's sake. Amen."

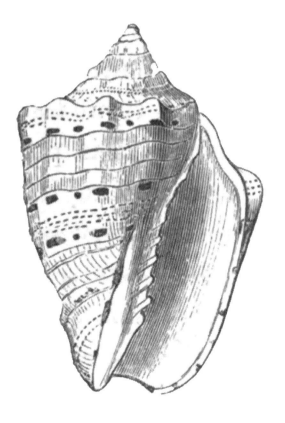

Voluta

Introduction

"Of all the tales of the sea, none are more pathetic than those which every now and again are related in curt language in the news columns of the daily press of the finding of messages written by those who far away at sea, the victims of some disaster, recognise the hopelessness of their position, and see on the horizon the dawn of eternity."
– Sheffield Evening Telegraph, 16 January 1893

One Thursday morning in late June 1899, an 11-year-old boy named William Andrews was playing on the beach near the Tunnels at Ilfracombe, North Devon. There he spotted a small tin floating in the water. The quarter-pound tin was marked "coffee and chicory", and was tied up with a piece of cork for buoyancy. Inside the tin was a note, written in pencil on a page torn from a pocket diary. The note was signed by able seaman R Neel and addressed to Mrs Abigail Neel in Cardiff. It read as follows: *"To my wife and children. The Stella is going down as I pen my last words. If I do not survive, go to my brother. Goodbye, my loved ones, goodbye."*

William took the message home, then passed it to the local newspaper. It was published in the next day's edition and, over the next few days, scores of other newspapers across Britain also printed the message. Its full meaning soon became clear. The *Stella* was a passenger ferry that had sailed between Southampton and the Channel Islands. It was wrecked in fog on the Casquets, north of Guernsey, in March 1899 with the loss of around 105 passengers and crew. No official passenger list was kept, and it was unknown whether an R Neel had been on board. Enquiries made at the given address in Cardiff found that a man named Neel had formerly lived there, but "was supposed to have gone to Bradford", where nothing else was known of him. Mrs Abigail Neel could not be traced.

The message found by William Andrews on that summer morning in 1899 was just one of hundreds washed up from the sea onto British and foreign shores in that year, and one of thousands during the busy Victorian and Edwardian steam and sail seafaring eras. These letters and notes were found on beaches and bobbing in water, in corked glass bottles and wax-sealed boxes, inside the mouths of codfish and in the bellies of sharks, carved on pieces of wrecked vessels and attached to the necks of seabirds. They told tales of foundering ships, missing ocean liners and shipwrecked sailors, and contained moving farewells, romantic declarations and intriguing confessions. Some solved mysteries of lost vessels and crews, while others created new mysteries yet to be solved.

In some cases, these messages would be passed directly to family members. In others, where the recipient could not be identified, or perhaps at the request of the sender, they would be forwarded for publication in the press. Major newspapers such as the *Times* of London and the *New York Times* often printed such messages, as did hundreds of national and regional newspapers across the world. They would often be published, as a semi-regular feature, in columns under the headline: "Messages from the Sea". It is from these columns that the messages in this book are drawn.

The earliest message from the sea is thought to have been sent by Greek philosopher Theophrastus around 310 BC. Theophrastus developed a theory that the Mediterranean was formed by an inflow of water from the Atlantic. In order to test his theory he dropped several notes sealed in bottles into the sea and waited to see where they ended up. If he ever received a response to his notes, it does not seem to have been recorded. However, messages in bottles would become commonly-used by government departments and research societies to study ocean currents, particularly during the 1800s and early 1900s.

On 30 November 1906, George Bidder of the Marine Biological Association in Plymouth released several bottles containing numbered postcards into the North Sea. On 17 April 2015, 108 years and 138 days later, one of the bottles, number 57, was found by Marianne Winkler at Amrum Island, Germany. It was recorded by Guinness World Records as the oldest (or technically the longest adrift) message in a bottle ever found.

Messages such as those sent by Theophrastus and George Bidder served a scientific purpose, but other notes placed in bottles, boxes and tins and thrown into the sea, such as the message from R Neel, were of a much more personal – and perhaps more vital – nature. The notion of the message in a bottle has come to attain a kind of romanticism, built perhaps on the allure of the exotic mystery its contents might reveal from a faraway place or a long-ago time. In the modern era, a found message is likely to have been written for fun or curiosity. But in the recent past, such messages served a much more practical and important function. For many seafarers, the message in a bottle was a legitimate and valuable method of communication – and perhaps their only means of contacting the outside world.

The hundred messages in this collection were

found between the years 1861 and 1915, a period spanning much of the Victorian era and the Edwardian era, through to the First World War. This was very much the golden age of the message in a bottle for three reasons. First, industrial and technological growth was leading to an increase in shipping, and there were an increasing number of vessels on the seas. Second, the absence of wireless telegraph and ship-to-shore radio meant seafarers had no alternative method of communication when out of sight of land. And third, better education and more readers led to a newspaper boom, which in turn created a demand for stories – for which the intriguing contents of messages in bottles often proved ideal.

Until the arrival of the wireless telegraph at the beginning of the 20th century, a ship that passed over the horizon and out of sight of land lost all communication with its home port for days, weeks or months at a time. Perhaps another vessel might spy the ship on the ocean and return with news of its location. Or a letter might be carried from a far-off destination to advise of the ship's safe arrival. But not all ships would arrive safely. Seafaring was incredibly dangerous. Hundreds of vessels were lost at sea each year, perhaps overcome by waves, dashed on rocks or engulfed in flames. A single storm could sink scores of vessels, or wipe out entire fleets. Those that didn't sink could be blown off course, become lost, and run out of food and water. Their crews might be left drifting in disabled ships, floating in lifeboats, or clinging to pieces of wreckage. In such a desperate situation, thoughts would inevitably centre on family and loved ones at home, perhaps hundreds or thousands of miles away. A brief message, written swiftly in the most hopeless of circumstances, might include a desperate plea for help, but would more likely comprise a tragic goodbye. Often, after disasters at sea, messages in bottles were considered to be what *Chamber's Journal* in 1880 called "the means of communication between the living and the dead".

Many of the messages in this collection represent the last words of stricken seamen who would never set foot on land again. They share several characteristics: details of a hopeless situation, a request to look after the family, often an apology, a plea to God, and a final farewell. Many share a relatively formal and straightforward tone. They would not be picked up by the intended final recipient, and might be published in newspapers, so the senders would restrain their emotions. Yet each message is uniquely individual: a different vessel, with a different home port, and a different family waiting for a different loved one to return from the sea. And not all are tragic tales. Some senders survived and returned home, often long before their messages were washed ashore.

Messages relating to ships were often passed to Lloyd's, the organisation that was responsible for maintaining shipping records for underwriters, merchants and other interested parties. Lloyd's had agents based in most major ports, and these agents would investigate messages from the sea with a view to updating their register. *Lloyd's Register* is a list of sea-going merchant ships of 100 gross tonnes or greater. Published annually since 1764, the register lists vessels until they are wrecked, sunk or scrapped. Some of the vessels named in these messages are listed in *Lloyd's Register*, which can generally confirm their loss. However, many other vessels are not listed in the register due to their not meeting the volume requirement. The vast majority of fishing vessels, for example, have a volume of less than 100 gross tonnes. In such cases there might be no official record of their existence, and their loss might go entirely unnoticed beyond their home port and the friends and families of their crews.

Some of these messages would have brought closure to the families of the crew and passengers of missing vessels. They brought terrible, heart-breaking news, but, after weeks or months of uncertainty, and the inevitable realisation that their loved ones would not be coming home, it was surely better to know what had happened, and perhaps to receive a loving message from their lost soul. In some cases, messages from the sea solved the mystery of vessels that had been missing without trace for several years, occasionally with hundreds of passengers on board. We know what happened to the *Titanic*, but what happened to fellow White Star liner the *Naronic*, or the Collins liner *Pacific*? Some of the messages included in this collection provide potential clues.

Other messages create their own mysteries, some of which can be solved, and some of which cannot. In some cases we simply cannot know whether the sender of a message describing their desperate situation happened to live or die. What happened to John Sorston, first mate of the steamer *Hiero*, which was going down in the Bay of Biscay? And did Antony Short, lost and starving off the coast of Australia, ever see land again?

Not all of the messages in this collection come from the sea. Some were found in rivers or lakes, and several were not sent from ships or boats. These messages in bottles contain confessions, suicide notes, or pleas for help. They concern murders, kidnappings, bodysnatching, and family secrets. Again, they present intriguing mysteries, and raise questions that cannot always be answered. Who was Charles Pilcher, and did he really murder Margaret Hutchinson and put her body in a well? Who was Elizabeth Granton, and did she find the secret of her birth that was hidden behind a picture of the Earl of Warwick?

And not all of the messages were found in bottles. Some were found in boxes, or scratched onto pieces of wood, or, in one case, etched onto a metal band that was wrapped around the neck of a recently-deceased albatross. One of the most remarkable messages collected here contains a poem written about a baby boy born on a long voyage from England to New Zealand. The message was found in a corked soda water bottle inside the stomach of an 11ft shark.

It is important to note that it is unlikely all of these messages are genuine. Hoaxes were common, with pranksters keen to see their missives published in the press. Newspapers would generally seek to verify the messages, making enquiries with Lloyd's and at the vessel's home port, and sometimes seeking to have a family member try to identify the sender's handwriting.

However, this was not always possible, and to refuse to publish an unverified message might be to deny the last wishes of a lost soul. Hoax messages "almost invariably give the name of a ship actually lost, in order to impart an air of verisimilitude to the story," said the *London Standard* in 1897. They were calculated, the paper said, "to awaken sad memories, especially in the minds of widowed women." The paper reckoned that hoax messages from the sea greatly outnumbered genuine ones, adding, "It is a pity the authorities cannot deal with the people who originate hoaxes of this kind."

The arrival of the wireless telegraph in the early 1900s, followed by the roll-out of ship-to-shore radio, gradually provided vessels with a lifeline of communication from the lonely isolation of the sea. The *Titanic* was fitted with a Marconi wireless telegraph system, and, on the morning of 15 April 1912, transmitted the Marconi "CDQ" Morse code distress signal, as well as the new international standard signal – "SOS". (Neither CDQ nor SOS are acronyms – they are simply distinct maritime radio signals.) Responding to the distress signals, the *Carpathia* was able to rescue more than 700 of the 2,224 passengers and crew. Some *Titanic* passengers did throw messages into the sea, but without the wireless they would surely all have perished.

Messages from the sea remain newsworthy. If a message in a bottle sent from one side of the Atlantic is found on the other, it will generally make local newspapers and television bulletins. Such modern messages retain a fascinating romantic allure, although their contents are often trivial, and will rarely be concerned with any great drama. The one hundred messages from the sea featured in this collection are from a lost era during which they represented a potential lifeline and were concerned with some of the biggest dramas imaginable. Together, they demonstrate the brave, lonely and fragile nature of life on the ocean waves.

– *Paul Brown*

A Note on the Text:

The messages in this book are reproduced as they were originally published in newspapers, with any inconsistencies in spelling, punctuation, capitalisation and date formatting left intact in an effort to best reflect the intentions of the senders.

Scallop

Cold Ocean

Found 15 July 1896
On the shore near Hoylake, Merseyside

In a bottle, written on a scrap of paper:

Struck iceberg—sinking fast in cold ocean—Naronic—Young.

The White Star Line cargo steamship *Naronic* left Liverpool for New York on 11 February 1893. On board were 50 crew, 14 cattlemen, ten horsemen and a cargo of livestock. The ship called at Point Lynas, Anglesey, and was never seen again. In March 1891, the steamer *Coventry* spotted two of the *Naronic*'s empty lifeboats in an area with large quantities of ice, close to where the *Titanic* would be sunk in 1912. At least four other messages in bottles relating to the *Naronic* were found, but none could be proven to be genuine, and the ultimate fate of the vessel remains a mystery.

Look After My Boy

Found 8 May 1871
Shediac, New Brunswick, Canada

Picked up on the shore in a bottle:

March 21, 1870. – City of Boston.

Ship sinking; over half full now. Good-by all. Look after my boy. Be gone in two hours.

THOMPSON.

The *City of Boston* was a Glasgow-built passenger steamship of the Inman Line. It sailed from Halifax, Nova Scotia for Liverpool on 28 January 1870 with 107 passengers and 84 crew. It never reached its destination and was never heard from again. A violent storm may have been responsible, although the ship's loss was also linked with the Scottish-born criminal Alexander Keith Jr, "the Dynamite Fiend", who conspired to blow up passenger ships with time bombs in order to collect insurance money.

Another message in a bottle alleged to be from the *City of Boston* was found in April 1870 at Staten Island, New York. *"As I write this note (perhaps my last on earth), I hear the wails and moans of my fellow passengers as they see the last vestige of safety lost and swamped in the deep,"* wrote a passenger identified by the partial signature *"James — nas"*. The *New York Herald* dismissed it, saying, "It is almost vain to entertain for a moment the idea that the letter is genuine, or, in fact, anything but a senseless and mean attempt on the part of somebody to create a sensation."

There were two Thompsons on board the *City of Boston* — a cabin passenger named John from Halifax, and a steerage passenger named William from New York. And there were more than a dozen passengers named James on board, including one listed as James McManaus.

Love From Hubert

Found 6 January 1907
On the shore near Ulverston, Cumbria

In a stout bottle, on a piece of ordinary envelope:

Finder please give this to relatives of Bertha Magnussam, Wavertree, Liverpool, England.

Love from Hubert, and good-bye.

Enquiries were being made by the Liverpool police.

The Body in a Well

Found October 1896
Near Shakespeare Cliff, Dover

In a small box, found floating at the foreshore by a lad named McKeen:

I, Charles Pilcher, murdered Margaret Hutchinson on November 23rd, 1870, afterwards putting the body in a well at Norwood, which, I believe, has never been found yet, and of late I can't sleep. I can always see her waiting for me at her pantry; that was our meeting place. To-night I have made up my mind to end my miserable existence by jumping over-board. My body will be good food for the fishes. I am not fit for anything else. So good-bye to everybody. I have no friends to weep for me. I am forsaken by all.

Enquiries at the police station in Norwood, south-east London, some 26 years after the alleged murder, found no recollection of a Margaret Hutchinson being reported missing, nor of a body being discovered in the district. "It was pointed out by the old inspectors that Norwood had entirely changed in character during the last quarter of a century," reported the *Canterbury Journal.* "Thousands of new houses had been erected, new roads made, and wells built over. Most wells had entirely disappeared since that time."

Inside a Cod

Found 13 February 1897
Buckie, Moray Firth

In a tightly-corked lemonade bottle, in the stomach of a large cod:

Schooner Lucio foundered eighty-six miles off Dunnet Head. God help us. J. Clunas, Ghent, Lerwick.

A catch of 5,000 cod was being gutted at James Gerry's fish-curing yard when this remarkable discovery was made. As reported by the *Sheffield Independent*: "On one large cod being opened a lemonade bottle, tightly corked, and bearing the name of Messrs J Hassack and Co, Elgin, was found in its stomach." Inside the bottle was a leaf of paper, torn from a pocket book, bearing a message from J Clunas. Dunnet Head is on the north coast of Scotland, near to John O'Groats and around 75 miles north of Buckie. The references to Ghent and Lerwick suggest the vessel could have been sailing from Belgium to the Shetland Islands.

Forgive Me

Found 1 June 1889
Off the Butt of Lewis, Outer Hebrides

In a small glass bottle:

19th May, 1856.

To Mrs Clunas, Burns Lane, Lerwick, Shetland.

Whaler Yoular. About my last hour. Forgive me for what I have done. May we all meet in Heaven.

John Clunas, Grinit.

Discovered while hauling in nets by the crew of the fishing boat *Isabella Reid*, this message, apparently more than 30 years old, was passed to the superintendent of customs. Newspapers did not comment on whether "Grinit" referred to a place or vessel, and did not speculate on whether John Clunas of the *Yoular* could have been related to J Clunas of the *Lucio*, whose message had been found two years earlier, and had also mentioned Lerwick in the Shetlands.

I Know I Cannot Escape

Found July 1861
Western coast of Uist, Outer Hebrides

In a bottle, the leaf of a pocket book, three inches by two inches, written on both sides in pencil:

On board the Pacific, from Liverpool to New York. Ship going down. Great confusion on board. Icebergs around on every side. I know I cannot escape. I write the cause of our loss that friends may not live in suspense. The finder of this will please get it published.

Wm. Graham.

The Collins Line steamer *Pacific* left Liverpool for New York on 23 January 1856, and was lost with all 141 crew and 45 passengers. The ship could accommodate 280 passengers, but was carrying a relatively low number on this winter crossing. It was thought to have sunk off Newfoundland. This note, found more than five years later, is the only record of its fate.

William Graham was a British sea captain travelling on the *Pacific* as a passenger. "The writer was evidently some person accustomed to the perils of the sea," commented the *Shipping and Mercantile Gazette*, "for it is difficult to understand how any person whose nerves had not been hardened by the presence of frequent and appalling dangers could have written with such manifest coolness in the immediate presence of death."

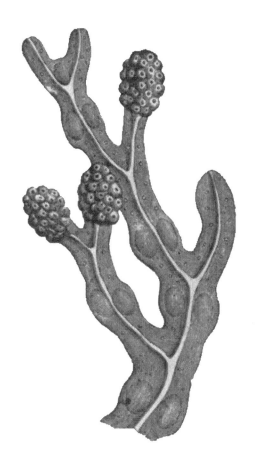

Bladder Wrack

A Pretty Little Boy

Found May 1873
Off the Scottish coast, near Dundee

In a soda-water bottle, corked and sealed with wax, inside an 11ft shark:

On board the Beautiful Star, Sunday, 1st September, 1872.

We have cross'd the line, and all's well. Last night the Captain's lady had a pretty little boy.

"Heaven bless the little stranger,
Rock'd on the cradle of the deep;
Save it, Lord, from every danger,
The angels bright their watch will keep.
Oh, gently soothe its tender years,
And so allay a parent's fears—
A father's love, a mother's joy;
May all that's good attend their boy."

ANNETTE GORDON.

The 11ft (3.35m) long shark was one of three large sharks caught within the space of a few weeks by Scottish fisherman. The shark's carcass was presented to the Dundee Museum, and gutted in front of a large crowd by the "dextrous knife of Mr James Dempster". Inside were found parts of cod, dogfish and seal, a man's bonnet, and a soda-bottle containing a note written "in a lady's neat hand".

The bottle was smashed open, and the note was read aloud to the spectators, who took pieces of the broken bottle as souvenirs. The man who took possession of the corked bottle neck, according to one newspaper report, "evidently considered that he had secured a great prize". He ran off with the bottle neck, pursued by a portion of the crowd.

The *Beautiful Star* was an Aberdeen-built clipper that sailed between Britain and Australasia. Enquiries found the ship in Lyttelton, New Zealand, where a Captain Bilton confirmed that the previous captain in command in 1872 had his wife on board, and "she was confined as stated".

Death Stares Us In

Found 22 March 1892
Dog Island, near Atlantic City, New Jersey

In a moss-grown, long-necked and tightly-corked bottle, hastily scrawled on wrapping paper, with $15 in cash:

The finder, whosoever it may be, will use this money as his own. We are sinking. Death stares us in —

"Here the note breaks off, and there is no signature, neither is the name of the vessel given," reported the *New York Times*. The bottle, picked up by fishing boat captain Samuel Chance, appeared to have been in the water for a "very long time".

Titanic Sinking

Found July 1912
Off Block Island, Rhode Island

In a bottle, on a wireless blank bearing the White Star *Titanic* imprint:

April 16—Mid ocean—help—on a raft—Titanic sinking—no water or food—Major Butt.

The sailors who found this message initially regarded it as a "ghastly joke", but the fact that it was written on *RMS Titanic* stationery brought them to believe that it was authentic. Archibald Butt was a well-known US Army officer, and a military aide to US president William Taft. He had boarded the White Star liner in Southampton, and was returning home after six weeks in Europe. The *Titanic* was sunk after colliding with an iceberg just before midnight on 14 April 1912. There are various accounts describing Butt's bravery in organising the lifeboats as the ship went down. Butt was one of the 1,521 passengers and crew who lost their lives. His body was never recovered. The date on his message suggests he had been adrift on a raft for more than a day.

In October 1912, a bottle was found in a fjord on the west coast of Iceland containing the message: "*I am one of them that were wrecked on the Titanic. — Harry Wilson.*" There was no Harry Wilson on the *Titanic*'s passenger or crew lists, although there was an Algernon Henry Wilson Barkworth, who survived.

A third message purporting to be from the *Titanic* was found in the summer of 1913, at Dunkettle, near Cork in Ireland. The message read: "*From Titanic. Good Bye all. Burke of Glanmire.*" 19-year-old Jeremiah Burke died on the *Titanic*, along with his cousin, Nora. His mother had given him a small bottle of holy water to take with him. The message washed up in that bottle just a mile from his home village of Glanmire.

It was speculated that Jeremiah could have thrown the bottle overboard while still in the Irish Sea, intending it to be a simple farewell to Ireland, with no knowledge of the disaster to come.

Torpedoed

Found November 1915
Hornsea, East Riding of Yorkshire

On a thin piece of wood, written in indelible pencil:

S.S. Membland torpedoed, engine-room port side.

Good-bye, dear.

The steamship *Membland* was lost while sailing
from Hull to Newcastle, with 22 men, two women
and a child. It was last seen off the Spurn Lighthouse, at the mouth of the Humber, on 15 February
1915. Wilfrid Wright, a carman, found the message
on the shore, and passed it to the coastguard. No
enemy ships had been sighted in the area, but
several vessels had been damaged by mines, and
the coastguard believed the message was genuine.

Drowned in Atlantic

Found August 1914
Larne Lough, County Antrim

In a stoppered bottle, written in pencil on a small square of blue paper:

24th March, 1913.

Drowned in Atlantic.

H. Scott, J. Caldwell, both of Dundee, Scotland.

The short note was passed to the postmaster, who forwarded it to the Dundee police.

Ready to Meet My God

Found November 1874
Off Key West, Florida

A slip of paper picked up by fishermen:

The schooner Lucie shipped from the coast of Georgia in August, loaded with lumber, and bound for Rio de Janeiro, (owned by Major Pollard, of St. Louis, and commanded by Capt. Hicks, of Boston) with Henry Mitchell, Mike Conely, John Meninger, and David Clark, of New-York, and four colored men. Was struck by a severe gale on the night of 27th September, some 330 miles off Rio de Janeiro, and had her mainmast and foremast carried away. She dipped and broke her bowsprit, and sprung a leak. All hands went to work to pump her out, and managed to keep her up until about nine o'clock the next morning, when she was dashed against a rock and went down.

We made a raft with the boards and put on some provisions but they were washed off during the day. Worn out with fatigue, Capt. Hicks and Mr. Meninger and one colored man got sick. We saw no vessel at all, nor an island near us. The poor sick men died the second day. Mitchell jumped off our little raft, and Conely was washed off. The negroes and myself are still alive, though weak, and the rough waves seem to toss us so I fear we shall not last long.

My dear wife Mary, and little babe live in New-York; may God bless them and take care of them. The Lucie was a 400-ton vessel, with three masts, but she is gone, and some of her gallant men with her, and we who yet live will, I fear, soon follow. I am ready to meet my God.

DAVID CLARK.

The *Lucie* had loaded with lumber at a sawmill near Brunswick, Georgia.

Harpa

Send Us Help or We Are Lost

Found 6 August 1883
Sea Isle City, New Jersey

In a bottle, picked up on the beach next to life-saving station 34:

Off Jersey coast. Lost at sea June 21, 1883, bark Atlanta, bound from Genoa to New-York. Have been without food for three days. Send us help or we are lost. Have buried Captain, mate, boatswain, and all but three sailors. Help us or we perish.

In July 1883 the US Board of Health reported three cases of yellow fever aboard a bark named *Atlanta*, which arrived at New Orleans (not New York) from Genoa after a journey of 97 days. The mate had died, and other crew-members had "dissipated". The ship had not visited any ports known to carry yellow fever. A few weeks later, Dr Holt, the president of the Board of Health, stated his opinion that "it was alcoholism, not yellow fever, from which the mate died and the others were made sick".

Not a Soldier

Found 3 June 1906
On the Thames shore at Hammersmith, London

In a corked bottle, written in pencil on a neatly rolled-up piece of paper:

I do hereby swear that I murdered Archibald Wakley at Westbourne-grove. Not a soldier; but as I am dead—or rather will be when message found—I will not let an innocent man suffer for my doings. If you go to xx Praed-street, Paddington, you will find a full confession and reason for deceased's death.

R. F. L.

xx Praed-street, W.

Archibald Wakley was a noted British artist who had exhibited at the Royal Academy. He was found murdered at his studio on 24 May 1906, having been battered to death with a ten-inch carpenter's hammer. Initial theories suggested Wakley had surprised a burglar, or had been killed by a female companion in a jealous rage over the pretty models he painted, although nothing appeared to have been stolen, and he was "not regarded as a ladies' man".

A witness claimed to have seen Wakley enter the studio with a uniformed soldier, and police found several sketches of soldiers, and a scrap of paper bearing the name of JT Walker of the Royal Horse Guards. The investigating pathologist had found a series of unusual puncture wounds that suggested Wakley had been kicked by an individual wearing spurred boots – as worn by horse guardsmen.

The police located JT Walker in Manchester, where he was attending a funeral, and returned him to London. It was reported that blood was found on Walker's uniform, which he attributed to a nose-bleed. Walker testified that he had met Wakley in Hyde Park some four months earlier, and had gone back to his studio, but had left after Wakley "made a suggestion to which he objected". Walker had an alibi for the night of the murder, and was not considered a suspect.

It was surmised that Wakley must have picked up another soldier in the park and brought him back to the studio, where the artist's "suggestion" had caused an "insane provocation" leading to "murder, but not wilful murder". The soldier was never identified. Neither was the message sender who claimed to be "not a soldier".

Police detectives made enquiries in Paddington (the house number at Praed Street was omitted from newspaper reports), but did not find any confession or further information relating to the message in a bottle. The *Daily News* concluded: "And there, for a time, perhaps for all time, the mystery rests."

Sixteen Days Without Water

Found March 1896
Cove Beach, Waipu, New Zealand

In a bottle, written in pencil:

A lost and starving man's request. - Should any person happen to find this bottle, will he be kind enough to make it known at some newspaper office that will report of what my fate has been. - i.e., lost at sea in an open boat off the coast of Australia. I am nearly exhausted for want of fresh water, and don't know where I am. Sixteen days without water is awful. God forgive me.

ANTONY W. SHORT.

Waipu is in the Northland Region of New Zealand's North Island, more than 1,200 miles from the coast of Australia.

Lost Three Men Overboard

Found 28 July 1883
Matagorda, Texas

In a bottle on the beach:

The finder will report this. We are now in a sinking condition, with all our boats washed away and the pumps all stopped up. We are off Cuba. Lost three men overboard. We have no fresh water. On board of the ship Cape of Good Hope. Feb. 22.

JOHN JOHNSON, Mate.

Matagorda is 1,200 miles across the Gulf of Mexico from Cuba.

I Expect My Turn Will Come Next

Found 17 June 1889
Near Gananoque, Ontario, Canada

In a bottle:

Captain of the Bavaria; help, the ship is sinking; all have been washed overboard but me. I expect my turn will come next. About 100 yards off Galoup Island, Lake Ontario.

The *Bavaria* was caught in a tremendous gale on Lake Ontario on 29 May 1889. It was on tow behind a steam barge with two other lumber schooners when its tow line sheared, and it was swept away at the mercy of the storm. The other boats survived, but the *Bavaria* did not. A witness later reported seeing the *Bavaria*'s Captain John Marshall clinging to the bottom of a capsized yawl, and another sailor clinging to timber, but could offer no assistance.

After the storm subsided, the *Bavaria* was found at Galloo Island, waterlogged but intact and upright.

All eight crewmembers were missing and their bodies were never recovered. John Marshall was married, and from Williamsville, Ontario. He was described as a brave and efficient sailor.

Don't Expect To Get Ashore

Found 6 September 1885
Charlevoix, Michigan

In a corked bottle:

July 25, 1885. Collided. The schooner Hattie Fisher went down off Point Betsy. The crew is in the boat this night. Don't expect to get ashore.

The *Hattie Fisher*, from Beaver Island, Lake Michigan, was owned by the island's priest, Father Peter Gallagher, and sailed by John E Bonner. Point Betsie is a lighthouse station on the north-east shore of the lake. After this message was found, enquiries among other Beaver Island sailors found that the boat had not been seen or heard from for some time.

Turbo

Have Sprung a Leak

Found 15 September 1896
Brittany, France

In a bottle:

Should this be picked up, please make inquiries or send G. Sortel, Esq., 50 Sixth Avenue, Philadelphia. I, William Eden, of the sailing schooner Vedette, write this at the very last moment, expecting my ship to sink every minute. Have sprung a leak in latitude 8 north, longitude 28 west. May God spare us. W. EDEN. Captain of Vedette, Philadelphia.

No record was found of any vessel named *Vedette* out of Philadelphia. There was no such address as 50 Sixth Avenue, and no resident of Philadelphia named G Sortel.

If Anything Happens

Found 6 January 1914
Bird Island, near Port Elizabeth, South Africa

In a well-corked black bottle, written in indelible pencil on a plain sheet of paper:

Waratah, Sept 6. 1909. - Ship in great danger. Rolling badly, Will probably roll right over. Captain going to heave her to. Later. If anything happens, will whoever finds this communicate this with my wife, 4 Redcliffe Street, South Kensington, London?

JOHN N. HUGHES.

The Blue Anchor Line passenger steamer *Waratah* was en route from Melbourne, Australia to London, England, via South Africa. It left Durban for Cape Town on 26 July 1909 with 211 passengers and crew on board. No trace of the ship has ever been found.

The message was described as "written very hurriedly". On 6 September, the date of the message, the *Waratah* would have been 48 days overdue.

There was no John Hughes on the passenger list, nor a Mrs Hughes at Redcliffe Street.

Several other messages apparently sent from the *Waratah* were found over the next few years, including one in a Castlemaine beer bottle that was returned for recycling to the Castlemaine Brewery in Freemantle, Australia, in November 1910. It read: "*May God have Mercy on us. We are now in a terrible Storm. 1st Officer, Waratah.*"

The waratah is a flower indigenous to New South Wales. The name was said to be cursed, as five previous ships named *Waratah* had been lost at sea.

Please Send This to My Aunt

Found 3 August 1881
Oak Beach, Long Island, New York

In a bottle:

YACHT MARGARET, July 14, 1881. We were wrecked in a heavy north-east wind off Faulkner's Island soon after the sloop Commerce left us; two of the crew were washed off while furling the jib topsail. Please send this to my aunt, and address Mrs. W. H. Parsons, Rye, N. Y.

No further record could be found of the loss of the *Margaret*.

Miss Charlesworth's Compliments

Found 11 January 1909
Wexford Bay, County Wexford, Ireland

In a tightly-corked mineral bottle:

To the press, police, and public of Ireland. Miss Violet Charlesworth presents her compliments and hopes she has not caused them any worry. Her journey from Cork to Rosslare has been very pleasant indeed, and she hopes to visit Ireland again soon. Au Revoir. This bottle was thrown through the porthole as our fine steamer was passing the great Tuskar Lighthouse. How powerful are these lights.

V.G.C.

Violet Gordon Charlesworth was a 24-year-old fraudster who, in January 1909, faked her own death in order to escape huge debts. Charlesworth had obtained tens of thousands of pounds from numerous sources by falsely claiming to be an heiress who would receive a £100,000 estate on her 25th birthday. With that date approaching, she faked her death by pretending to fall from her motor car over a cliff and into the sea at Penmaenmawr, North Wales.

Newspapers reported various apparent sightings of Charlesworth after her death, at Holyhead boarding a steamer for Ireland, in Bray, and then in Wexford. Detectives at nearby Rosslare regarded the message as a hoax. By the end of January, Charlesworth had been found, alive and well, in Oban, Scotland. She was charged with conspiracy to obtain money under false pretences, and sentenced to five years' hard labour.

Trois Freres

Found 3 March 1874
Staten Island, New York

In a corked bottle:

Le vaisseau Trois Freres, de Calais, France, fut naufrage,
Mars 3me, 1874, lat. 49.45, lon. 23.54.

VICTOR VANDEBROUCQUE.

[Translation:]

The ship Three Brothers, of Calais, France, was wrecked,
March 3rd, 1874 lat. 49.45, lon. 23.54.

VICTOR VANDEBROUCQUE.

The *Trois Freres* was described as a French sailing ship, with no further details provided.

Rewarded For Their Kindness

Found 8 November 1895
Cape Charles, Virginia

In a securely sealed bottle:

Off Cape Fear, July 19, 1895, bark Julia A. Marks, leaking badly, nearly sunk; bound from Baltimore to Cuba; may have to leave here any time. If not heard from, please report this to Collector of Customs at Baltimore, where we cleared from. She hailed from Bath, Me. Please inform my family in Portland. The one finding this will be rewarded for their kindness.

Capt. John Marks.

The message was found on the beach by a drug clerk named AH Bowie. Newspapers noted that no vessel named *Julia A Marks* had recently sailed from Baltimore, and no vessel by that name was mentioned in the Record of American and Foreign Shipping. However, the writer of the message may actually have given the name of the vessel followed by his own name as captain: "*Julia A*, Marks".

Farewell Forever

Found January 1888
Near Sable Island, Nova Scotia, Canada

Picked up in a bottle by the captain of the government steamer *Newfield*:

Newfoundland, Nov. 12 1887.

DEAR PARENTS: I come to bid you farewell forever. I will soon be in the other world; not alone, however, for we are 890 passengers in terrible despair. Only one-half hour to live, and then farewell. Do take courage and think no more of me.

L. Linther of St Nicholas, Meurthe.

Saint Nicolas de Port is a town in Meurthe-et-Moselle, Northern France. There is no record of a passenger ship being lost in November 1887.

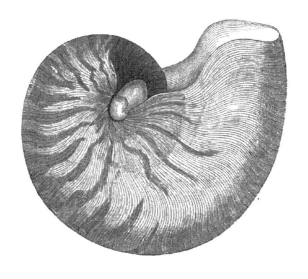

Nautilus

All Well

Found 30 August 1869
San Buenaventura Beach, Ventura, California

In a water-tight seal-skin bag, written in the margins of a printed form, much mutilated:

[Printed text, in five languages:]

WHOEVER finds this paper is requested to forward it to the Secretary of the Admiralty, London, with a note of the time and place at which it was found; or, if more convenient, to deliver it for that purpose to the British Consul at the nearest Port.

[Handwritten text:]

HMS Erebus and Terror. 28 of May 1847. Having wintered in 1846-47 at Beechey Island in Lat. 74* 43' 23" N. Long. 91* 39' 15" W. After having ascended Wellington Channel to Lat 77* and returned by the West side of Cornwallis Island. Sir John Franklin commanding the expedition. All well.

[Written at foot:]

Party consisting of 2 officers and 6 men left the ships on Monday, 24th May, 1847. G. M. GORE, Lieut. CHAS. F. DesVOUX, Mate.

[Written in margins:]

1848. H. M. ships Terror and Erebus were deserted on the 22nd April, five leagues N. N. W. of this, having been beset since Sept. 12, 1846. The officers and crews, consisting of 105 souls, under the command of Captain F. R. M. CROZIER, landed here - in lat. 69* 37' 24", lon. 98* 4' 15". A paper was found by Lieutenant IRVING under the cairn supposed to have been built by Sir JAMES ROSS in 1831, four miles to the northward, where it had been deposited by the late Commander GORE in June, 1847. Sir JAMES ROSS' pillar has not, however, been found, and the paper has been transferred to this position, which is that in which Sir J. ROSS's pillar was erected. Sir JOHN FRANKLIN died on the 11th of June, 1847, and the total loss by deaths in the expedition has been to this date 9 officers and 15 men. F. R. M. CROZIER, Captain and Senior Officer. JAMES FITZJAMES, Captain H. M. S. Erebus. And start on tomorrow, 26th, for Back's Fish River.

Explorer Sir John Franklin's fourth and final Arctic expedition set sail from Greenhithe, England, on 15 May 1845, with 24 officers and 110 men. Franklin was attempting to navigate the Northwest Passage, connecting the Atlantic and Pacific via the Arctic Ocean. The entire expedition was lost. The last recorded sighting was in late July 1845. The first traces of the expedition were found by search parties in 1850.

Numerous searches took place over the following decades, and the first note was found in 1859. Other Admiralty Forms were found, with duplicated updates scrawled in their margins, on land and at sea. It is thought that, with their ships icebound, the starving men set out onto the ice, where they were driven to the cannibalism of their deceased colleagues, before eventually succumbing to the elements.

This message was found on San Buenaventura Beach by lumber merchant James Daly. "How strange that after 21 years their message should at last come to shore in California," commented the *San Francisco Chronicle*, "and that the telegraph should flash its news and import to those at home who had long forgotten them."

100 Horses

Found 27 August 1889
East of Lossiemouth, Moray

In a small tin box, a slip of paper:

Steamship Lady Anne, foundered at sea, N.N.E.

20 men, 100 horses, 41 passengers.

To my mother at 56 Back Street, Findhorn, Mrs Smith.

Findhorn is a village in Moray. The message was handed to a Mr Brander, an agent for Lloyd's.

Spanish Steamer Opened Fire

Found June 1889
Off the Carnarvonshire coast, north Wales

In a bottle:

S.S. Enore.

3 p.m., April 24th, 1898; sixty-five miles W.S.W. of Smalls Lighthouse. At four a.m. this morning a Spanish steamer bore down on us, and fired three shots; two went through our side above water. We stopped, and they sent a boat and nine or ten men to ransack our ship, taking everything of any value, and leaving many of our crew wounded. After the boat left, the Spanish steamer opened fire on us, and had thoroughly riddled our starboard with shot holes. Nine of my crew are killed altogether, and the ship is now sinking very fast. It is impossible to float another fifteen minutes. The small boats were smashed by Spanish sailors. We have no hope left at all. Good-bye.

C. McNeill.

Smalls Lighthouse is located on the Smalls Rocks, some 20 miles west of the Pembrokeshire coast. 24 April was the day before the beginning of the four-month Spanish-American War. Some newspapers referred to the message as a "war despatch".

Lloyd's stated that there was no such steamer named the *Enore*. "Of course there isn't," responded the *Cardiff Evening Express*. "What remained of that gallant barque, after the Spaniards had done with it, disappeared beneath the pitiless waves at a quarter-past three pm."

Run Over by a Steamer

Found July 1904
Floating off Stavanger, Norway

On a piece of bark:

Borregaard — I can tell you she is sinking between England and the Orkney Islands. We were run over by a steamer. This is the last I can inform you.

The Norwegian steamer *Borregaard* was sailing from Fleetwood to Sarpsborg, and was last seen off Dunnet Head in Caithness. No other trace of the ship or its 13 crew was ever found.

The Sea Is Offal Heavy

Found October 1892
Broadsea, Fraserburgh, Aberdeenshire

In a bottle:

Oct. 7th, 1892.

At Se. Smack Prince Wales.

Dear Mother.

We R lying to in a horaken of wind of Orknes, and the sea is offal heavy. Harly posabel to us to live in it. If I never see you anie mor God will provid for you. The two other men is keeping up with a good harth; love to all from your son, CHARLES GILBERTSON.

Newspapers called this misspelled message a "characteristic letter".

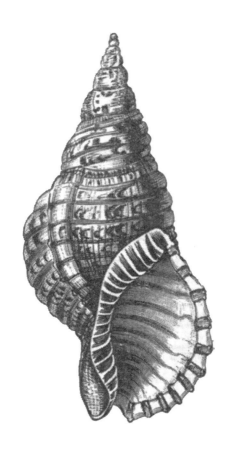

Triton

MESSAGES FROM THE SEA

Lifting of the Body

Found February 1883
On the beach at Trondra, Shetland Islands

In a bottle, on a torn piece of paper:

This bottle was thrown into the water at Stirling, in the river Forth, on the 15th July 1882, by one of the men who were concerned in the lifting of the body of the Earl of Crawford. The body is now, I think, rotted into clay. We lifted it with the intention of selling it, but it was published so soon that we buried it to get it out of the way.

Further text appeared to have been torn off before the message had been placed into the bottle. Alexander William Crawford Lindsay was the 25th Earl of Crawford. He died in Florence, Italy, in 1880 and his body was returned to be buried in a private chapel at his family home at Dunecht House, near Aberdeen. In December 1881, it was discovered that the body had been stolen — apparently some months beforehand.

The body was eventually found in July 1882, buried in a shallow grave, by a rat-catcher named Charles Soutar. Although Soutar denied any involvement, and was not considered capable of having carried out the crime alone, he was charged with grave-robbing and sentenced to five years in prison.

May the Lord Comfort My Mother

Found January 1893
Holderness coast, East Riding of Yorkshire

On a plank of wood:

Caller Ou run down by unknown steamer—Dawson.

No more time, sinking. May the Lord comfort my mother.

The *Caller Ou* left Hull 14 month prior to the message being found and was never seen again. Dawson was an apprentice on the vessel. The unknown steamer was never identified.

Mutiny

Found July 1914
Norwegian coast

Washed up in a bottle:

Angus — all hands — mutiny — collision with foreign barque.

The handwriting was identified as belonging to the second engineer of disappeared Hull trawler the *Angus* by his landlady, who produced other letters from him as evidence. The landlady thought the note to be genuine, but could not explain the word "mutiny" as the crew were "very friendly".

Know I Died Happy

**Found September 1866
Ventnor harbour, Isle of Wight**

In a corked wine bottle, stamped "Patent, Powell and Co., Bristol":

Her first voige to England.

June 17, 1866.

The Spanish Queen, bound for Bristol with timber from Quebec, having left on the 5 of March, and owing to the rough weather, which has lasted 9 days, the old ship leaks like a sieve, and we are settling down fast. All hands are out at the pump, and the captain is ill upon deck, but is riting a note to put it in a flask. It is my last wish if this bottle is picked up that it may be published in some papers, as I have a Dear father and mother, and I should like them to know I died happy. There is no hope for us. I shall not throw this over till the last.

Hands in number, 23.

I remain yours.

GEORGE J. MILLS.

The message was retrieved by William H Whitewood, who waded into the harbour up to his knees. It was photographed by Mr Frederick Hudson, and passed to the coastguard. Mr Hudson wrote to the *Times*, offering to send copies of the photographs to the parents of George Mills, saying, "They may prove some slight consolation to them in their bereavement."

Laden with Paraffin

Found July 1867
Sound of Sleat, west coast of Scotland

In a bottle, on a slip of paper torn from a pocket diary:

March, Thursday, 21. Sprung a leak in the Minch—ship Diana, of Hull, laden with paraffin; no hope; ship going down. Master, John Tod.

The Minch is a strait between the west coast of Scotland and the Western Isles, north of the Sound of Sleat. In April 1867, it was reported that several casks of paraffin had drifted ashore around the Sound of Sleat.

Dying Blessing

Found 26 December 1889
Whanganui, New Zealand

In a corked bottle, written in pencil:

Ship County of Carnarvon, September 3, 1889.

Anyone who should find this bottle will earn the dying blessing of three men, who do not expect to live an hour, by letting our friends and relations know our fate. We are sinking fast. All hands but us three were washed overboard last night. We were dismasted, and the binnacles and everything washed away by one sea. Every sea washes over the deck fore and aft. I don't know where we are, but by the skipper's reckoning at midday yesterday we were about 1000 miles from New Zealand. We have been sinking fast ever since the squall struck us. May God help us, for we may sink at any minute.

George Wright.

The other men with me are Vincent Wallace and James King.

The *County of Carnarvon* of Liverpool left Newcastle, Australia, for Valparaiso, Chile, on 5 June 1889 with a crew of more than 20. In September, a battered lifeboat bearing the ship's name was found on the beach at Taku, New Zealand. Locals said the boat had come ashore during a heavy storm. The colonial government despatched the steamship *Hinemo* to search for survivors, but none were found.

Delesseria

Thirteen Shipwrecked Refugees

Found 18 September 1887
North Fremantle, Western Australia

On a rusty tin band, fitted around the neck of a recently-deceased albatross:

---

13 naufragés sont réfugiés sur les îles Crozet, 4 Août, 1887.

[Translation:]

13 shipwrecked refugees are on the Crozet islands, 4 August, 1887.

The Crozet Islands make up a small French-owned archipelago in the southern Indian Ocean, 3,500 miles from Fremantle, where a lad walking on a beach found this message. It was punched into a rusty tin band, nine inches long and two inches wide, wrapped around the neck of a dead albatross, which had apparently flown the great distance over several weeks before expiring on arrival.

Australian authorities sent a search vessel to the Crozets, but found no trace of shipwrecked sailors, and the message became regarded as a hoax. However, in January 1888, a French search vessel found a further letter on the uninhabited Pig Island.

The letter stated that 13 shipwrecked men from the ship the *Tamaris*, having exhausted their provisions, had left the small island on 13 September to head to the larger Possession Island. No trace was found on Possession or any other Crozet island.

"Whether they were drowned in their effort at escape remains as yet unknown," commented the *Pall Mall Gazette*. "But this much seems too unfortunately certain, that the life of the noble bird was sacrificed in vain."

Drifting for Hours

Found 14 August 1891
On the beach near Benton Harbor, Michigan

In a bottle:

We, the undersigned, are passengers on the Thomas Hume. The schooner's hold is rapidly filling with water, and we have no hope of escape. We are on the St. Joseph course and have been drifting for hours. We have friends in McCook, Neb., and Eckhart, Ind. Please notify them of our fate.

FRANK MAYNARD,

WILBUR GROVER.

The *Thomas Hume* was owned by Hockley and Hume of Muskegon, Michigan. It was lost on Lake Michigan on or around 10 May 1891 with seven men on board. No trace of the vessel was ever found.

Leaking Badly

Found 23 July 1883
Off Long Island, New York

In a bottle, picked up by Captain Chase of the steamer *General Bartlett*:

Schooner Smuggler leaking badly. Seine boats gone. Can't keep afloat much longer. If this is found send news to Gloucester. Off Cape Elizabeth, July 15.

From Gloucester, Massachusetts, the 1877 schooner *Smuggler* was regarded as one of the most handsome schooners ever built. Although the *Smuggler* did become grounded on a ledge in July 1888, it was freed on the following day, and proceeded on its journey apparently undamaged. This message was therefore either an over-panicked dispatch or a hoax.

A Fearful Day

Found 7 April 1889
On the beach at Sunderland

In a bottle:

March 20, '89.

My Dear Friend,

We have met with a fearful day; I never thought it was to be my last. I hope whoever gets this will send it to my sister. Our ship is sinking—three feet of water every hour. We are 70 miles east from the Bell Rock. We are coal loaded. Dear sister, I hope you will write my love to Mary and let her know my fate. No more from your loving brother J. Ford. Good night for ever, my dear sister, Jane Ford, No. 21 Smith Court, Aberdeen.

Barque Mary Hopp, Sunderland.

The Bell Rock is off the coast of Angus, Scotland, 50 miles south of Aberdeen, and some 140 miles north of Sunderland.

Everything Is Destroyed

Found 28 February 1877
Near Crail, on the Fife Ness headland, Fife

In a bottle, a letter much blotted and destroyed by sea water, written in bold characters:

To Tonsberg, Norway. Schooner Bay, Tonsberg, 25th Dec., 8 o'clock, morning. We are now in a sinking condition within sight of the Bell Rock, outside the river Tay. We have had both boats smashed and carried away, and cannot, therefore, make an attempt to come ashore. We have experienced great hardships during heavy gales in the North Sea. Greater part of rails, stanchions, and bulwarks are away. We have been labouring constantly at the pumps for three days, and the forecastle and the cabin are full of water. Everything is destroyed, and we have had but little to eat. We now put our trust in a merciful God, and if it is our fate to die we hope to arrive at a heavenly throne. The crew is otherwise all well, and ask to be remembered to the dear ones at home.

H MATHISEN, Captain of Schooner Bay.

The message was translated from Norwegian by Mr Patterson, the consul for Norway and Sweden in Dundee, and passed by him to the ship's owners. The *Bay* was sailing from Newcastle to Tonsberg laden with coal and bricks, with a crew of six hands. Locals recalled a "fearful" storm at Christmas 1876 that had left large quantities of wreckage floating about the mouth of the Tay, near to the Bell Rock. The presumption was that "many vessels" had been lost in the storm.

Two days after newspapers printed the message came confirmation that the *Bay* had been one of those vessels. However, the crew had survived. An earlier report revealed that the *"Bai"* had been within sight of the Norwegian coast when it was caught in the gale and driven back across the North Sea. With the ship waterlogged and sinking, the captain had run it ashore among rocks at Crail. The vessel was spotted by the coastguard, led by Commissioned Boatman Smith, who used the rocket apparatus life-saving device (which fired safety lines from the shore to stricken vessels) to rescue all six hands. The *Bay* was wrecked, but the crew were returned home safely to Norway.

Detained on Island

Found April 1906
Floating in the Mississippi near Muscatine, Iowa

In a bottle, written on a small piece of wrapping paper in feminine hand:

I am detained on island short distance above Lyons by two tramps.

Rescue me.

Anna Sherman.

The Muscatine fisherman who found this message floating near the Iowa shore initially thought little about it. However, after showing it to friends, he came to think it might have been "written in earnest", so handed it to the police at Clinton County, around 50 miles upriver from Muscatine. The town of Lyons no longer existed. It was annexed into the city of Clinton in 1894, although locals continued to use its name.

Clinton police procured a launch and set out to search for Anna, but found all of the islands above Clinton to be submerged under the swollen Mississippi. "The affair may only be a prank of some girl," said a local newspaper, "but it may prove to be a kidnapping case, and may lead to the discovery of some unlawful deed."

Kept There by Force

Found 29 July 1901
Bath Beach, Brooklyn, New York

In a bottle:

July 27, 1901.

Dear sir or madam—If you find this note I wish you would tell the police that I am in a cabin in Bath Beach and kept there by force. I remain yours truly, B. VIOLET CULLEM,

No. 209 East Fourteenth street, N. Y.

The message was found on the beach at the foot of 17th Avenue by a young woman, who handed it to an employee of a nearby hotel. It was then passed to police, who made a search of the area and took a launch out to search yachts. No trace was found. "The message is believed to have been placed in the bottle by a thrilling newspaper reporter who was anxious to get a sensational story," said the *Brooklyn Daily Eagle*, which reported that local residents were "considerably annoyed" following a spate of bogus newspaper stories centred on Bath Beach, and considered the message a "pure fake".

The address given with the message was a boarding house for theatrical groups, but there was no resident named Violet Cullem. However, as the *Daily Eagle* reported, "A few days ago, a young woman whose Christian name was Violet had made arrangements to board there, but she did not arrive."

Trochus

Gone Down in the Bay of Biscay

Found 12 August 1861
Lamlash Bay, Isle of Arran

In a bottle:

Gone down in the Bay of Biscay, the screw-steamer Hiero. Have taken to the boats but don't expect to see land again. May the Lord have mercy on us!

John Sorston, First Mate, July 17, 1861.

There was no record of the *Hiero* in *Lloyd's Register.*

A Cargo of Cotton

Found 26 August 1866
Slains Castle, Cruden Bay, Aberdeenshire

In a bottle:

Ship City of New York. Sailed 6th December with a cargo of cotton, bound for Granton. Went out of her course 13th Jan. Boats all lost. Ship going down. God have mercy on our souls.

GEORGE ADAMS, carpenter.

This message was picked up by a gardener at the 16th century Slains Castle, more than a hundred miles north of the *City of New York*'s stated destination of Granton, Edinburgh. An Inman passenger liner also named *City of New York* was reported safe.

Cannot Get Away

Found 8 February 1877
Birsay, Orkney

In a bottle secured to a lifebuoy:

St. Kilda, January 22, 1877.

The Pete Mubrovacki [sic], of Austria, 886 tons, was lost near this island on the 17th inst. The captain and eight of the crew are in St. Kilda, and have no means of getting off. Provisions are scarce. Written by J. Sands, who came to the island in the summer, and cannot get away. The finder of this will much oblige by forwarding this letter to the Austrian Consul in Glasgow.

The Austrian barque *Peti Dubrovacki* left Glasgow for New York on 11 January 1877. It capsized in bad weather six days later, around eight miles west of St Kilda in the Outer Hebrides. Seven crewmembers died, and nine survived to reach the remote archipelago. The survivors were taken in by St Kilda's 75 or so residents, and shared the islanders' dwindling rations, mostly consisting of grain seeds.

On 30 January, fearing starvation, a visitor named John Sands placed a message in a bottle, tied it to a lifebuoy from the *Peti Dubrovacki*, rigged up a small sail, and placed his "St Kilda mailboat" into the sea. Nine days later, it washed up at Orkney, more than 200 miles away. On 22 February, the navy gunboat *Jackal* arrived at St Kilda, the bad weather subsiding for just long enough to allow the rescue of the Austrian seamen and John Sands, and the delivery of biscuits and oatmeal for the islanders.

John Sands was a Scottish journalist and artist who had been living on St Kilda for several months. He returned to the mainland "barefoot and penniless" on board the *Jackal*, and later published a book about his experiences on the island, *Life on St Kilda or Out of this World*. His original St Kilda mailboat is something of a local legend, and the sending of similar mailboats has become an island tradition.

MESSAGE FROM THE SEA.

"THE SHIP IS SINKING."

A bottle was recently found on the beach, in Partage Bay, in the Peninsula of Alaska, containing a message written on a sheet of the Northern Pacific Steamship Company's letter-paper, of which the following is the exact wording: "Ss. Pelican, Lat. 50 degrees, N., Long. 175 degrees. W. The ship is sinking. We are leaving her in frail boats. Please report us.—M. T. Patterson, Chief Officer. Port Townsend, Washington. U.S.A." The Pelican was an iron screw schooner, the registered owner being Mr. Whealler, of Messrs. Dodwell, Cardiff, and Co., of Hong Kong. She sailed from Tacoma in October, 1897, bound for Taku, and from then until now she has not been heard of.

Message from the Pelican, 1899 (see page 119)

SS City of Boston, disappeared 1870 (page 20)

SS Pacific, sunk by icebergs 1856 (page 27)

Major Archibald Butt and the RMS Titanic (page 33)

Murdered artist Archibald Wakley (page 41)

SS Waratah and crew, missing 1909 (page 51)

Fraudster Miss Violet Charlesworth (page 54)

MESSAGES FROM THE SEA

Sir John Franklin and HMS Erebus and Terror (page 60)

Lifting of the Earl of Crawford's body (page 69)

Bell Rock Lighthouse, Angus (page 83)

St Kilda, Outer Hebrides (page 93)

HMS Atalanta, disappeared 1880 (page 115)

SS London, sunk in Bay of Biscay 1866 (page 132)

MESSAGES FROM THE SEA

Sea Messenger, Vanderbergh invention (page 143)

Crew of whaler Snowdrop return home 1909 (page 159)

THE LOSS OF THE NARONIC.

A MESSAGE FROM THE SEA.

Information was received at the office of the White Star Company, Liverpool, yesterday, that a bottle had been picked up on the shore near Hoylake containing a scrap of paper, on which was written—"Struck iceberg—sinking fast in mid ocean—Naronic—Young." The Naronic, a cargo steamer belonging to the White Star Company, disappeared on her maiden voyage to New York three years ago, and her fate has remained a mystery. The Company are sceptical as to the message.

A MESSAGE FROM THE SEA.

A bottle has been picked up at Broadsa, Fraserburg, containing the following characteristic letter:—"Oct. 7th, 1892.—At Se.—Smack Prince Wales.—Dear Mother.—We R lying to in a horaken of wind of Orknes, and the sea is ofal heavy. Harly posabel to us to live in it. If I never see you anie mor God will provid for you. The two other men is keeping up with a good harth; love to all from your son, CHARLES GILBERTSON."

Messages from the Naronic, found 1896 (page 19),
and the Prince Wales, found 1892 (page 67)

Washed Away During Gale

Found 26 September 1895
In the harbour at Poole, Dorset

In a bottle, on a foreign telegram form:

Owner, ship Sarah Jane, Liverpool. Ship sprung a leak on 17th August off St. Ives. Ship sinking, and boats washed away during gale of 2nd inst.

James Goodenough, 20 New-street, Isle of Dogs.

This message was fished out of the harbour by a revenue cutter. The writing was described as being "in clear running hand" and "evidently that of a well-educated person". Police enquiries found there was no New Street on the Isle of Dogs. A Board of Trade inspector identified a vessel named *Sarah Jane* that traded between Birkenhead, across the Mersey from Liverpool, and Millwall, on the Isle of Dogs. However, there were no reports of that vessel having encountered difficulties, so the message was labelled by the press as a "cruel hoax".

We Are In Great Distress

Found 5 March 1861
South Shields

In an oil bottle, written in pencil on a parchment leaf from a pocket book:

Feb 8, 1861. Brig Juno, of Yarmouth.

Dear Friends.

We are in great distress. We have been working at the pumps night and day. When you find this card we are no more. Our fore and main masts are gone.

J.P.

The *Dublin Evening Packet* published this message under the headline "Melancholy Intelligence".

A Harbour I Will Never See

Found February 1865
Near Silloth, Solway Firth, Cumbria

In a bottle:

My dear wife,

My vessel, the Caledonia brig, of Belfast, is about to go down. I am running her for the Isle of Man; but a harbour I will never see. My men are all reconciled to their Heavenly Father's will. My dear wife, I am leaving you in sore distress, with a heavy charge, but I know that the Lord will fulfil his promises to you; you have long sought Him. I have my Shipwrecked Mariners' Fund cards all with me. I now leave you, my dear wife and children, to the Lord. Them that find this letter hoping they will send it to Belfast to the News-Letter Office.

John Nisbett.

A year after this message was found, at a meeting of the Shipwrecked Mariner's Society in Belfast, it was announced that "a widow named Nisbett, residing in Belfast, whose husband was a subscriber to the society, obtained relief for herself and children to the amount of £13 9s 3d, and will have a small grant annually while the children are unable to provide for themselves".

Mrs Nisbett had provided the Society with her husband's message as proof of his death.

Dog Whelk

Nora Will Get Over It In Time

Found July 1867
Off the west coast of Africa

In a bottle:

Ship Dover Castle, Jan. 13, 1867.

Mr Alfred Dawes begs to inform his friends, at 23, East Cliff, Dover, that the ship is about to go down; he begs that his friends will pay all his bills, and trusts that Nora will get over it in time. The ship is two days' sail from the Line, outward bound. Anybody who gets this will oblige Mr. Dawes by putting it in The Times newspaper. And now as I have not much longer to live, believe me yours,

A. DAWES.

The message was picked up from the sea by Kroomen (West Africans recruited into the British Royal Navy) and passed via George Blackshaw at the Company of African Merchants' Factory in Liberia to *The Times* in London.

The Secret of Her Birth

Found February 1869
Cullenstown, County Wexford, Ireland

In a bottle, on soiled, torn paper with no date:

The finder of this is to tell Elizabeth Granton, of Ashton Grange, on the borders of London, E.C., that the secret of her birth will be found behind the picture of the Earl of Warwick, in the drawing-room, and receive the blessing of a dying man.

Interest in this message was, according to the *Belfast News-Letter*, "awakened by the fact that there is a lady in the case, and that it has a romantic air about it." The abbreviation "EC" suggests London's East Central postcode area, from an era before UK postcodes had numbers added to them. However, Victorian gazetteers do not list an Ashton Grange in or around London.

Seen Whale

Found September 1894
River Carron, central Scotland

In a bottle:

11th August, 1894.

Seen whale. Boat capsized; drowning off Dunbar. To my wife, Jeanie Bryce. God help you. Forget and forgive.

D. Bryce, Bo'ness.

The River Carron runs into the Firth of Forth, at the mouth of which sits Dunbar. Borrowstounness, commonly known as Bo'ness, is also on the south bank of the Firth of Forth.

Fearful Hurricane

Found 28 April 1880
Junction of Weaver and Mersey, near Runcorn

In a bottle, written very legibly in pencil:

H.M.S. Atalanta, March 16. Fearful hurricane, dismasted, going down fast, off Lizard. H. Smith, boy.

The *Atalanta* was a British Navy training frigate, commanded by Captain Francis Stirling. The ship left Bermuda for Portsmouth carrying 281 men and boys on 31 January 1880. It was never seen again.

In April 1880, the Navy sent the Channel Fleet to search for the *Atalanta*. No trace was found, and it was thought the ship must have sunk in the area now referred to as the Bermuda Triangle, where heavy weather had been reported at the time of the disappearance. However, the Lizard, mentioned in this message, is a peninsula — notorious for ship-wrecks — on the south coast of Cornwall. If the message was genuine, the *Atalanta* had sailed for more than 3,000 miles from Bermuda, and had sunk within 200 miles of its destination.

There were four Smiths on board the *Atalanta*, although none with the initial H. One RW Smith was named among the list of the missing as "boy writer".

On 5 May 1880, a small piece of wood was found at Dalkey near Dublin bearing a short message: "*HMS Atalanta going down, with all hands on board, in latitude 48.60. Signed J. Steward.*" There was no one named J Steward on board, although there was a J Cooper listed as "boy steward". The given latitude runs around 50 miles south of the Lizard.

Clinging to the Mast

Found 15 March 1897
On beach between Hartlepool and Seaton Carew

On a piece of strong paper:

Foundered off Holy Isle, the S.S. Elsie. Six lives lost. Four survivors clinging to the mast

---

The remainder of the message was torn away, with only a single further word visible: "*soon*". The Holy Island of Lindisfarne is a tidal island off the Northumberland coast, around 80 miles north of the beach where the message was found.

No More Whisky

Found August 1912
Saint-Brevin-les-Pins, western France

In a bottle, on Prince Line headed notepaper:

Ship in distress. No more whisky on board. Please refill bottle and return it.

As gleefully recounted by Singapore's *Straits Times*, this light-hearted message was "an example of real distress at sea" — just four months after the sinking of the *Titanic*. It was apparently found by a French bather at Saint-Brevin-les-Pins, near Saint-Nazaire, who summoned a gendarme, then the chief of police, and then the mayor, none of whom could translate it from English. The message was hurriedly carried, by the bather still in his swimming costume, to the mayor's office, where a traveller's phrase book failed to help. It was eventually translated by the British vice-consulate. The Prince Line was a major steamship company that had been founded in the north east of England.

In Frail Boats

Found 15 May 1899
Portage Bay, Alaska

In a bottle, on a Northern Pacific Steamship memorandum form used by a Hong Kong shipping agent:

S.S. Pelican. Lat 50 N, Long 175 W.

The ship is sinking. We are leaving her in frail boats. Please report us.

M.T. PATTERSON, Chief officer.

Port Townsend, Wash., U.S.A.

The *Pelican* was a Glasgow-built Northern Pacific steamer. It left Tacoma, Washington, for Taku, near Beijing, on 3 October 1897 and was never seen again. The ship was listed by Lloyd's as missing on 9 February 1898. It was thought to have sunk during a gale.

Then in September 1911, a schooner named *Saucy Lass* returned from the Bering Sea to its home port of Victoria, British Columbia, with news of the *Pelican*. Islanders on Akutan, one of the Alaskan Aleutian Islands, had found four skeletons lying on the rocks just above the water line. The skeletons appeared to be wearing Northern Pacific Steamship uniforms. It was speculated that the unfortunate crew of the *Pelican* had managed to reach shore, "only to perish of exhaustion".

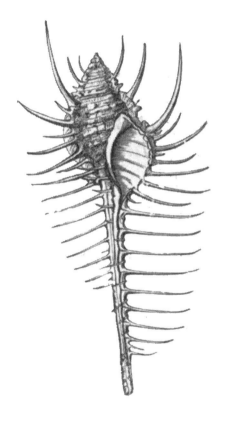

Murex

Shipwrecked on Sandbank

Found February 1878
In a burn near the Firth of Forth

In a bottle:

Annaberga, of Plymouth. December 11th, 1877. Andrew Raine, Joseph Malley and Jules Kahm, survivors. Shipwrecked on sandbank. May God have mercy on our souls.

Even the location at which this message was found is a mystery, being named by different newspapers as "in the Parkburn Forth" and "at Parkburn, Forth". Others gave the location simply as "near Dunfermline". Parkburn does not appear on contemporary maps, but it was most likely a burn or small river near to the Firth of Forth. Confusingly, some newspapers said the name of the vessel was *Annaborga* not *Annaberga*, the home port was Liverpool not Plymouth, and the survivors' names were Andrew Paine, Joseph Dally and Jules Kupin. Perhaps unsurprisingly, no further record of the vessel or its crew could be found.

Six Inches Per Hour

Found 17 June 1879
Tayport Harbour, Fife

In a bottle:

In latitude 58.20 N.; in longitude 1.20 E.

Three days without water; ship making 6 inches per hour; cargo shifted; intends to leave the ship the first opportunity.

Mary Ann, Portsoy. John Cumming, mate. — 25/5/79.

The given coordinates suggest the *Mary Ann* was around 150 miles east of its home port of Portsoy, Aberdeenshire.

To The Foaming Deep

Found January 1861
On the beach at South Shields

In a bottle:

North Sea, Feb. 2, 1860.

Dear Friends,

When you find this the crew of the ill-fated ship Horatia and Captain Jackson, of Norwich, is no more. We left Archangel on the 8th of January, all well; on the 2nd of February we hove to under close-reefed topsails, after scudding before the gale for 10 days; we have not been below for six days. A Norwegian brig hove to for our assistance. Four men got into the jolly boat, but after leaving a sea struck her, and sank her, and the four men were lost. Our crew consisted of eight men, master and mate, second mate, and two boys. When I am writing this, I have just left the pumps. We are not able to keep her up — 8 feet of water in the hold, and the sea making breach clear over her. Our hatches are all stove in, and we are worn out. Our master made an observation today. We are in 60 North lat.; wind, N.E. I write these few lines, and commit them to the foaming deep in hopes they may reach some kind-hearted friend who will be so good as to find out the friends of these poor suffering mortals. I am a native of London, from the orphan school — John Laing, apprentice. We are called aft to prayers, to make our peace with that great God, before we commit our living bodies to that foam and surf. Dear friends, you may think me very cool, but, thank God, death is welcome. We are so benumbed and fatigued that we care not whether we live or die. John Ross, John Thompson, James Lee, Jos. Brig took the boat on the 21st of January.

William Ham, chief mate; Thomas Wilson, second mate; John Laing, and Frederic Maff, apprentices.

Although this detailed message was widely published around the UK, no further information regarding the *Horatia* (or *Horatio*, according to some newspapers) was found.

Living on Raw Penguins

Found 24 November 1878
Wellington, New Zealand

In a sealed bottle:

H.M. screw corvette Firefly, Captain Harmer Jones, wrecked November 2, 1878, on the Auckland Isles. All lives saved except three A.B.'s and second engineer.

Signed, H. Jones, commander, H. Leslie, first-lieutenant.

Send relief at once. Provisions all exhausted. Living on raw penguins. The lord help us.

Found on a beach behind the New Zealander Hotel by the son of the hotel owner Frank Mountain, this curiously detailed message was regarded as a "silly hoax".

Looking Out For a Sail

Found September 1871
Gulf of Mexico

Written in pencil:

Off East Coast of Brazil, Jan. 21, 1871.

This is to certify that we three are the only survivors of the English ship Lilian, lost on the night of the 15th of this month. We have now been drifting in an open boat for six days, suffering hunger, thirst, and hardships which none but those that has experienced can illustrate. We have been looking out for a sail since the ship went down. What became of the captain and the rest of the men God can only tell.

JOHN THOMAS, Second Mate.

MICHAEL DOOLEY, Seaman.

JOHN DUGER, Seaman.

Some newspapers gave the *Lillian* three Ls. "It may be a hoax," one said, "but if not it is of so much importance as to be thought worthy of publication."

Crew on Half Whack

Found 10 March 1900
Parrot Bay, West Indies

In a corked bottle:

Ship Samoena, of Greenock, latitude 21 ½ degrees north, longitude 37 degrees west, May 19th, 1899, from Portland, Oregon, to Queenstown, for orders; 130 days out, and no provisions aboard. Crew on half 'whack', living on cargo of wheat and do not expect to ever reach port. If this is picked up, please send word to E.S. Fardon, 11, Agnew-street, Lytham, Lancashire, England.

The message was delivered to the Lytham address on 19 April 1900 with a postscript: "*Found by Robert Higgs, overseer of Parrot Bay, on the beach at S.C., on the 10th of March, 1900.*" "S.C." suggests South Carolina, or perhaps the Seychelles, although newspapers said the message was "cast ashore at Parrot Bay, West Indies". "Whack" was a sailor's food ration, so "half whack" meant half rations.

The *Samoena* had left Portland on Christmas Eve 1898, encountering a heavy storm, then drifting for several months. When provisions ran out, the crew ground up the ship's cargo of wheat with a coffee mill to provide sustenance. In a moment of despair, in May 1899, able seaman Edward Stanley Fardon wrote this note and dropped it into the sea.

Almost a year later, when the message arrived in Lytham, it was received by one Edward Stanley Fardon. Several weeks after being given up as lost, the *Samoena* had arrived home safely with all hands. Fardon, who it was reported was no longer a seaman, was said to be "one amongst the few men who have been privileged to read, after many days, his 'last message'."

Good Soil

Found August 1897
Ellesmere Port, Cheshire

In a bottle, on faded paper:

Zoe, S.S., lost in South Pac Ocean. Compass broken. No means of telling in what latitude we are. Captain dead through yellow fever. Only four alive. Provisions to last several months. Lost all count of time. Island good soil, but no tools. God help us!

"We could enumerate fifteen distinct reasons why this precious document must have been bogus, but it would be an insult to the intellect of a congenital idiot to detail them," said the *London Standard*. "But seriously, it is a pity the authorities cannot deal with the people who originate hoaxes of this kind."

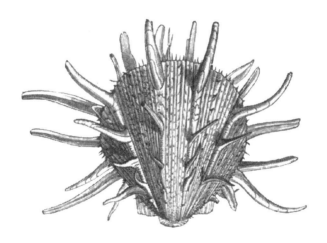

Spondylus

Too Heavily Laden

Found 12 February 1866
Near Quiberon, Brittany, France

In a bottle:

H.J. Dennis to Jno. Dennis, Esq., at Great Shelford, nr Cambridge. Farewell, father, brothers, sisters, and my little Edith. Ship London, Bay of Biscay, Thursday, 12 o'clock noon. Reason—Ship too heavily laden for its size, and too slight a house over engine room, all washed away from deck. Poop windows stove in—water coming in everywhere. God bless my little orphan. Request to send this, if found, to Great Shelford. Storm, but not too violent for a well-ordered ship.

This was one of six messages contained in three bottles that washed up at the same spot on the French coast. It was found 32 days after the sinking of the SS *London*, a British steamship that was sailing from Gravesend, England to Melbourne, Australia. The ship left Gravesend on 13 December 1865, carrying at least 239 passengers and crew, and laden with 400 tons of railway iron and coal. As it sailed past Purfleet on the Thames, a seaman on the riverbank was reported to have remarked that this would be its last trip. "She is too low down in the water," he said. "She'll never rise to a stiff sea."

After sheltering from heavy weather at Plymouth, the *London* crossed the English Channel and headed into the Bay of Biscay. There it was caught in a terrible storm, which led its Captain Martin to order a return to Plymouth. However, huge waves swamped the low-sitting ship, and swept away all but one of its lifeboats. The *London* sank, stern first, on 11 January 1866, with those on board reported to have sung the hymn *Rock of Ages* as they went down. Nineteen survivors escaped in the only remaining lifeboat. At least 220 people died, with some reports also including several unregistered stowaways, plus a baby that was born on board.

An inquiry found the main cause of the tragedy to be overloading. The loss of the *London*, and several other vessels, prompted a government commission led by MP Samuel Plimsoll to introduce a mandatory load mark line painted on ships' hulls to indicate levels of buoyancy and prevent overloading. The mark is now known as the Plimsoll Line.

Henry Denis was a widower who left a young daughter, "now entirely an orphan". The six messages, described by the *Era* newspaper as "sad documents from the dead, farewells and blessings of sons to their parents, and of husbands to wives and children", were passed to Lloyd's. A further message was found washed up on Brighton beach, supposedly from the Shakespearean actor Gustavus Vaughan Brooke, who went down with the *London*.

In September 1867, a bottle was found in Exmouth harbour containing a tailor's bill on the back of which was written a message from one Francis Day: "*Lost in the ship London. Advertise to my friends that I have £3,000 in the London and Westminster Bank.*"

Down to Plimsoll's Mark

Found 12 January 1877
On the shore at Occumster, Caithness

In a bottle:

My Dear Wife and Son.—We are laid-to in the North Sea, about one hundred miles westward of the Holman, with our main hatch stove in and gangways gone. The sea is fearful; it is washing in and out of the main hatchway, and washing the linseed out of the hold. It happened at four a.m. this morning. My dear, we have the boat swung out all ready for lowering, but we dare not for the sea. There is no water in the after hold, and the engine is going ahead to pump the water out, but I am afraid it is to no purpose. I don't think we shall live the night out. Pray to God to forgive us our sins, for we have many. My dear wife and son, it is a painful thing to write to you both and say that I expect every moment to be my last. The ship was too deep—down to Plimsoll's mark. Ships ought not to be allowed to load so deep. Good day, and God bless you all; and I hope He will protect you. Tell John to be a good boy, and keep honest and sober.—Your affectionate husband JOHN COOK, Chief Mate S.S. Wells, of Hull, 130 Day Street, Hull. P.S. Kind love to all.

The *Wells* left the Baltic Sea port of Memel (now Klaipeda) for its home port of Hull on 17 December 1876. When it did not arrive, "the gravest fears" were entertained for the ship and its crew of 22 men. This message confirmed those fears.

After it was published in newspapers, the ship's owner, Mr Alderman Wells, sought to assure the public that the *Wells* had not been overloaded, and had in fact been carrying less cargo than usual since the addition of its Plimsoll Line. Then, having initially regarded the letter as "perfectly genuine", the owners revised that opinion and said it could not have drifted to its finding place, and must therefore be a hoax.

However, wrapped around the cork of the message's bottle was found a small piece of newspaper torn from the *Newcastle Journal*. The piece was forwarded to that newspaper's office in Newcastle upon Tyne, where it was confirmed it had been taken from the edition dated 29 November 1876. The Wells had sailed out of the Tyne on its way to the Baltic on 29 November 1876. This was regarded as "rather curious confirmation" that the message was genuine, and that the *Wells* was indeed lost.

In Sight of Land

Found February 1894
Kilbaha, County Clare, Ireland

In a bottle:

To Mrs Captain Keogh, Isle of Wight. Friday Evening.

My dear Louisa,

I am in sight of land (Blackets) this evening; lost our deck load of timber, and am thinking our gallant barque will be lost too. Farewell, dear Louisa and the children, till I meet you in heaven.

Your loving husband, Henry Keogh.

Kilbaha is a small fishing village on Ireland's Atlantic seaboard, a journey of more than 500 miles from Henry Keogh's Isle of Wight.

Lost Off Lundy

Found May 1875
Milford Haven, Pembrokeshire

In a bottle, stoppered with an iron belaying pin and oakum, written on a piece of paper:

---

6 April, 1875. John Limerick, Schooner, Isabel, Cork, lost off Lundy in a fog. All hands perished, except one.

Lundy is an island in the Bristol Channel, around 40 miles south of Milford Haven. The *Western Mail* printed this message under the headline "Waif from the Sea".

A Sober, Industrious Young Man

Found March 1897
On the shore of the Potomac, Washington DC

In a peculiar-looking bottle:

March 22.

Will the person that finds this be kind enough to spend 2 cents and let my folks know that I am no more. I have tried four months to get work, but fail. The only thing I could do was work for my board, and I had no where to sleep. I was a sober, industrious young man.

TEDY BENSEMAN

527 Elmwood avenue, Columbia, S.C.

A small boy named Willie Tucker fished this message in a bottle out of the Potomac River while walking along the shore near the Washington Monument grounds. No clothing or other effects were found on the shoreline. Analysis of the "small, vertical" handwriting suggested the writer was fairly well-educated and, in the opinion of the police, "may possibly be white". A police boat made a search of the area, but plans to drag the bottom of the river were abandoned.

News of the find was sent to the address in Columbia, but no reply was received. "There is some speculation as to whether the whole thing is a hoax," said the *Washington Times*, "however, no motive can be shown for any attempt at deception, and for this reason the supposition is that there may be a man at the bottom of the river."

Hermit Crab

Condition Sink

Found 15 October 1892
On the shore at West Granton, Edinburgh

In a bottle on the scrap of an envelope, written in pencil:

May 17, 1892. Steamship Amelia. Condition sink—lat. 40; long. 63.4. McGrath.

The given latitude and longitude coordinates appear to be inaccurate. The message was handed to the police.

Sea Messenger

Found 25 November 1870
On the coast near Penzance, Cornwall

In an airtight metal case with a boat-like bottom and a metal flag mounted on top:

Schooner Yacht Cambria, Nov. 26, 6.30 p.m., 1870, in lat. 49 18 N, long. 7 82 W.

Dear Sir,

We launched a 'sea messenger' to the deep with this enclosed. We have just finished taking third reefs in foresail and mainsail, as there is every appearance of a dirty night, but glad to say we have a fair wind—rather a new thing for us to have this passage. We had 15 days' strong easterly winds, with high seas, from the 3rd to the 18th inst. We passed to-day, at 3.30 p.m., the American ship Enoch Talbot, bound up channel. There is every appearance now of strong westerly winds. We are going ten knots.

Yours truly,

R.S. TANNOCK, Master.

This was one of six messages contained in the "sea messenger", launched from the *Cambria* as an experiment to test the new invention. Painted on the front of the metal case were instructions for it to be delivered to the nearest Lloyd's agency, where an agent would open the case and forward the letters to their respective addresses. The case was duly delivered to Messrs Mathews, the Lloyd's agents for Penzance, and this letter was forwarded to the address of a newspaper correspondent in Portsmouth.

"This 'sea messenger' is the invention of Mr Julius Vanderbergh, of Southsea, as a means of preserving papers, &c., from a ship lost, or in imminent danger of being lost, at sea," explained the *Chelsea News and General Advertiser*. "If not seen and picked up by some passing vessel, the messenger will be almost certain eventually to drive on the land, and may thus convey ashore the tale of some helpless ship, whose loss, with all on board, could by no other means be learnt." The newspaper said that the sea messenger's capture near Penzance, and the subsequent delivery of its letters, was "evidence of perfect success".

1702

Found June 1903
Karpathos, Greece

In a hermetically-sealed bottle:

1702.—The ship clown, on board which we were, found-ered at the beginning of October, 1702. She foundered so quickly we barely had time to get off on the raft, on which we now are, without food or drink. Whoever finds this paper is begged, in the name of humanity, to for-ward it to the Government. One of the castaways.— Manter.

The two-century-old message was found by a Greek fisherman on a "lonely part" of Karpathos, and sold to a local doctor. Karpathos (or Carpathos) is one of the Sporades islands in the south-eastern Aegean Sea. It is referenced in Jules Verne's *20,000 Leagues Under the Sea* as the home of the sea god Proteus.

Norwegian at Sea

Found September 1893
Washed ashore at west of Shetland Islands

In a bottle:

Norwegian at sea: 50min, 16 sec. west.

Ship foundering. All hands leaving in ship's boats. If this message found advertise in the Norwegian papers.

Christian Halversten, master.

The message was dated 24 June 1893, suggesting it had been at sea for more than two months. The name of the ship was not provided.

The Walrus is Sinking

Found 27 June 1911
On the beach west of Pointgarry, North Berwick

In a bottle, legibly written on a piece of paper:

Will the finder of this message communicate with 25 Kirkgate, Leith? The Walrus is sinking, Good-bye.

J. Flint.

According to the *Scotsman* newspaper, enquiries made in Leith "failed to throw any light on the message".

A Token of My Respect

Found 8 July 1914
Bondi Beach, Sydney, Australia

In a bottle, written in indelible pencil on pieces of linen, apparently torn from a man's shirt, with two silver cufflinks tied to the cloth:

To the Finder of this Bottle, if Found.—I am the third officer of the (in English) Shima Maru, Japanese trader. We struck a derelict 7 miles west of Loyalty Island, 4 a.m., on 16/5/14. We took boats, and we lost bearings. We are now on an island. Skipper and mate are dead, second mate ill. There's only I and third mate, and seven others, all weak. We are sailing in a few days in hopes of finding an inhabited island. Sir, will you do me a kindness. Let my people know I am alright up to writing this. Sir, if you make this known, please don't make their names known, or that of my young lady. Sir, please accept the links as a token of my respect for the kindness which I know you will now do me. I hope that I may see you if I come out alive, and thank you personally. Tell them, sir, you will, for humanity's sake. Don't let them think I did not try, but I can only hope. Good luck, sir. I wish I were you now. Goodbye.

This was one of three messages found in a bottle by a boy named RE Moore and passed to Captain Hacking at the Navigation Department. A woman's name and full address were given in the message, but they were not printed in newspapers in accordance with the writer's wishes. Captain Hacking thought it "improbable" that a bottle could have drifted from the Loyalty Islands, an archipelago some 1,200 miles north-east of Sydney, in the space of seven weeks, but he nevertheless informed the Japanese Consul. No vessel named *Shima Maru* had been reported missing. However there was a 112-ton wooden steamer of that name, built in 1898, listed in *Lloyd's Register*.

I Was Shot Last Night

Found 25 April 1897
Floating in Snake River at Weiser, Idaho

In a bottle:

April 10, 1897.

I was shot last night by an unknown party. I am mining on Snake river at Big Bend. I am dying.

Yours, W. C. Cook.

Snake River's gold deposits attracted many placer miners, most of whom lived and worked alone along the river. "Ten days ago an attempt to murder one of these miners was made at another point in the river," reported the *Ravalli Republican.* "In this instance, the victim was left for dead but survived. The motive was robbery, and if there is anything in this story told by the bottle, it is probably another case in which a lone miner has been attacked for the gold which he has accumulated."

Bear Hotel

Found 7 February 1912
South coast of Iceland

In a bottle, written in pencil on a slip of paper:

Harry James Kelsall, passenger on S.S. Canada, Sept. 2nd, 1911, Sunday, Liverpool to Ottowa, late proprietor Bear Hotel, Newcastle-under-Lyme, Staffs, England.

Public house landlord Harry Kesall sailed to Canada on board the White Star–Dominion steam liner named *Canada* in August 1911. On Sunday 2 September, having sailed for around 1,200 miles, and "in a spirit of sportiveness", Kelsall threw overboard his message in a bottle. He returned from Canada in December, and thought nothing more of the message.

In March 1912, "to his infinite surprise", Kelsall received a letter from the British Vice Consul in Reykjavik, Iceland, enclosing his message on its slip of paper "in an excellent state of preservation".

"Naturally, Mr Kelsall is very proud of the possession of such an interesting and unique memento," said the *Staffordshire Sentinel*, "and it is his intention to have the letter and slip of paper framed."

Cockle

Highland Lassie

Found July 1905
At the mouth of the River Mersey

In a bottle:

Highland Lassie. No hope. Out in a boat off Tuscar.—

Smith.

The message was found by a Liverpool workman bathing at the mouth of the Mersey. The *Highland Lassie* was a Nelson Line cargo steamer that had left Swansea for the River Plate on 10 December 1904 and disappeared without trace. One of the ship's crew was named Smith. Tuscar is a set of rocks with a lighthouse off the south-east coast of Ireland.

Dreadfull Weather

Found April 1883
Holm, Orkney

In a bottle, written in pencil on a sheet of hand-made paper taken from the leaf of a log book:

Dreadfull weather. Steamship Marie Stuart sinking off Hull. Captain washed overbord three days ago. Eleven feet of water in the hold, masts all gone, and in another hour she will go down. God help us. Farewell.

The steamer *Marie Stuart*, from Leith, left Burntisland on the Firth of Forth on 6 March 1883 and was never seen again. This message was found by farmer James Harcus, who saw a bottle floating in the sea and waited for it to come ashore. "The writing is neither dated nor signed," reported the *Liverpool Mercury*, "and seems to be written by a seaman, and not an officer, as two words are misspelled – 'dreadful' having an extra 'l', and 'overboard' spelled without the 'a'." The message was forwarded to the owners of the *Marie Stuart*.

Turned Over Sunday Night

Found 2 June 1902
Picked up 45 miles east of Halifax, Nova Scotia

In a bottle, written on a scrap of paper:

Steamer Huronian turned over Sunday night in Atlantic. In small boat, 14 of us.

The Allan Line steamship *Huronian* left Glasgow for Saint John, New Brunswick, on 7 February 1902. That month was notable for severe weather conditions, with raging storms and strong gales over the Atlantic. The *Huronian* was carrying 56 crew, one passenger, and a cargo of coal. It disappeared without trace, despite the efforts of a Royal Navy search team. Conditions were so bad that one of the search vessels, the HMS *Thames*, was almost lost in a storm. In March, several bedsacks used by steerage passengers on Allan liners washed ashore near Halifax. Then, in June, this message was found in the water.

In January 1907, almost five years after the *Huronian*'s disappearance, a second message in a bottle was found at Castlerock, Northern Ireland. The message read: "*Huronian sinking fast; top-heavy; one side under water. Good-bye mother, and sister.— Charles McFall, greaser.*" It was confirmed that a greaser or engine fireman named Charles McFall had been on board the *Huronian*, and the message was regarded as genuine. One newspaper hoped it could be passed to McFall's family, "to be preserved as a touching memento of one of the many mysteries of the sea".

All Hands Will Perish

Found February 1879
On the sands at Craster, Northumberland

In a bottle:

The Mary Jane, of Dover, bound from Glasgow for New Zealand, was wrecked 300 miles off the coast of England. It is supposed all hands will perish. There is a heavy sea, and crew in small open boats.

T. SNAITH, captain.

The *Berwickshire News and General Advertiser* said this message stated the *Mary Jane* "was wrecked 300 miles off the coast of New Zealand", not England, and therefore concluded it must be a hoax as it could not have drifted such a distance. But this seems to have been based on a transcription error, as in the first publications of the message, in the *Sunderland Echo* and *Shields Gazette* a week earlier, the ship "was wrecked 300 miles off the coast of England", and there was no suspicion of a hoax.

Remains of the Dundee Whaler

Found 8 March 1909
On the beach near Coldingham, Berwickshire

In a bottle:

Captain or anyone who receives this message shall receive the remains of the Dundee whaler Snowdrop, collided with iceberg. No hope. 14th November 1908.

The *Snowdrop* left Dundee on 23 April 1908 to hunt whales in the Davis Strait, between Greenland and Canada in the Arctic Circle. The ship was the smallest whaling vessel in its fleet, with a crew of just ten, including the ship's owner (and harpooner) OC Forsyth Grant, its captain and expert Arctic navigator James Brown, and a 17-year-old Eskimo named Inear. The ship was last reported safe and well on 8 June 1908. Nothing else was heard until the arrival of this message, which confirmed suspicions that the *Snowdrop* had been lost in the Arctic.

Then, on 16 September 1909, with the ship missing for over a year, a telegram was received from Indian Harbour, Labrador. The telegram reported the arrival there of a young man named Alexander Ritchie, an able seaman, and a member of the crew of the *Snowdrop*. Ritchie explained that the ship had been lost in the Frobisher Strait on 18 September 1908, but the crew had escaped into a boat, which had drifted for several days before reaching Baffin Island. There, the crew had found an Eskimo village, where they spent the winter "on the verge of starvation" but cared for by the friendly natives. In the spring, Ritchie had crossed the hundred-mile part-frozen strait between Baffin and Labrador by foot, dogsled and boat in order to seek help.

The schooner *Jeanie* sailed to Baffin Island to rescue the crew, and returned to Labrador on 25 September 1909. However, one man was missing. John Morrison had set off with Ritchie to cross the strait, but had suffered severe frostbite and gangrene that required one foot and part of the other to be amputated, with the procedure carried out by Eskimo women. When the *Jeanie* arrived to rescue them, the crew had not seen Morrison for several months. A three-day search was fruitless, and it was surmised he was "in the interior with natives".

The crew of the *Snowdrop* returned to Dundee in October 1909, 18 months after they had left. There were several attempts made to find Morrison during subsequent whaling trips to the Arctic. A year later, in October 1910, the *Dundee Courier* reported the tragic news: "Poor Morrison is Dead!" While in the care of the natives, the gangrene had returned, and a further amputation had been performed, from which he had not recovered. It was thought that Morrison had died in December 1909, two months after his crewmates had returned home.

If Our Remains Be Found

Found 18 September 1889
Off Eastbourne, East Sussex

In a bottle, written in pencil on a sheet of paper:

Firefly, private yacht. February 9, 1889, off Denmark. Dear Friends whom happens to read this, we were a party of four hands all told, when we were run into by a two-master, and I am now writing these lines, which I hope will come into some person's hands who will send help to us as soon as possible. But if by any chance any of our remains be found please let our friends know at Hastings, Sussex, England, and also the—

This abruptly-curtailed message was picked up by fisherman Phillip Swain floating in the English Channel more than 400 miles south-east of Denmark but less than 15 miles from Hastings, which the *Times* said was "somewhat remarkable". A local correspondent confirmed the *Firefly* was missing, and, said the *Times*, "there is little doubt she was wrecked and her crew drowned."

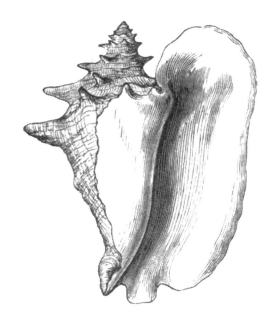

Strombus

God Help Us

In a bottle, a note scribbled in pencil:

Schooner Lizzie foundering off Corsewall Point. God help us.

Corsewall Point is 40 miles south of Troon on the west coast of Scotland. No Scottish vessel named *Lizzie* was known to be missing, and the message was initially assumed to be a hoax. However, it was subsequently revealed to be the last dispatch from a Northern Irish vessel, from Kircubbin, County Down, across the North Channel.

The *Lizzie* left Maryport, Cumbria, on 22 November 1898, and was due in Kircubbin on the following day. However, it was caught in a severe gale, and was last seen heading north, apparently to seek shelter from the storm. A week later, a lifeboat bearing the *Lizzie*'s name was washed ashore near

Larne, County Antrim, around 25 miles from Corsewall Point. "No doubts are now held that the vessel foundered in the heavy gale, which, it will be remembered, caused a lot of damage to shipping at the time," reported the *Glasgow Herald*.

The *Lizzie* had a crew of four hands, led by Captain McWhirr, who left a widow and eight children, "most of whom are young".

Steamer Combat

Found 29 July 1875
In the sea near Barrow-in-Furness, Cumbria

In a securely corked bottle, indistinctly written on a scrap of old newspaper:

Gone down off the coast of Ireland the steamer Combat, with all hands.

Captain Yates.

The undated message was found by a girl named Ann Holme. "The writing seems to have been hurriedly done," remarked the *Yorkshire Post*, "and the paper is much worn and soiled."

Consigned to the Thames

Found 11 January 1905
On the Bucks Bank of the River Thames

In a bottle:

F. James, East-street, Walworth.

Has consigned his body to the River Thames at Bourne End.

January 8th, 1905.

Signed, F. JAMES.

The message was found by Buckinghamshire Police, and a Police Constable Heater took a boat out onto the river, but found no trace of a body. Several fishermen had been on the banks of the river on 8 January, and none had seen anything suspicious. No person had been reported missing from East Street in Walworth, South London. It was considered that the message "might have been put there for a lark".

However, on 30 April the body of an unknown man was found in the Thames near Cookham, across the river from Bourne End. PC Heater recovered the body. The coroner said there were no signs of violence, and the likely cause of death was drowning. The body had been in the water for several weeks.

Found on the deceased were two wrist straps, several buttons, a piece of pencil, a broken match box, a glazier's diamond and a workman's cheque. There was no name on the cheque. PC Heater made enquiries at several local glazing firms, but the man could not be identified. At an inquest held at the Bel and the Dragon Hotel, a jury returned an open verdict of "found drowned".

Ship Ariosto

Found 18 June 1890
River Ribble, Lancashire

In a sealed bottle, written in lead pencil on the leaf of a pocket book:

June 4th. Ship Ariosto of Liverpool. Ship sinking. No hope. God bless us all.

J. Stewart, captain.

The message was found by a Preston Corporation workman while dredging at the south bank of the Ribble. Although published at face value in scores of British newspapers, it was regarded by the *Preston Chronicle* as a hoax. A ship named *Ariosto* was in service, transporting passengers and cargo between Gothenburg and Hull, but it was not lost until 1916, when it was scuttled by torpedoes during the war.

New York Stock Exchange

Found February 1900
Cahersiveen, County Kerry, Ireland

In a bottle:

Lost off sloop Nancy, bound from New York to Liverpool. Sailed in dinghy without food or water or rum. Kindly let New York Stock Exchange know that four of us—C. M. K., Jim Thomas, Mrs Thomas, and myself have perished.

Herbert E. Ward. Prudential Insurance Co. of America, Home Office, N.J.

Herbert E Ward was the son of Leslie D Ward, the vice president of Prudential Insurance, based in Newark, New Jersey. Herbert's wife was named Nancy, like the sloop. Newspapers noted the couple were well-known members of "Newark's exclusive social set". However, there were no reports of Herbert being lost at sea. When his father died in 1910, leaving an estate worth $4 million, obituaries noted that Herbert was already deceased. Records show Herbert died in 1905.

Going to My Doom

Found 21 February 1913
At the mouth of the Thames

In a bottle, a paper containing two messages:

[On one side of the paper:]

Dec. 17, 1904; S.S. Nutfield. 5, Hardwick-street, South Shields, England. Dear Wife and Children,—All the time I have been writing this I am going to my doom. I hope you will look after the children, and that Willie is a good lad to you. Best love to all. Let my father and mother know.—W. Howard. x x x

[On the other side:]

S.S. Nutfield.—To whoever may pick this up.—Please make it known that our ship is doomed. We have a very heavy deck load on, and are looking for every minute to be our last. Good-bye to all.—J. Slater, South Shields. Dec. 16, 1904. We are in the English Channel.

The *Nutfield* was lost with all hands in the English Channel more than eight years before this message was found. William Howard, the ship's donkeyman engineer, and J Slater, the engine fireman, were well known among the merchant seamen of the Tyne. Slater's message is dated 16 December and Howard's 17 December, suggesting the ship may have sunk over a period of time spanning late night and early morning.

The messages were found on the south shore of the Thames by a man named George Johnson, who forwarded them to Mrs Howard in South Shields. Mrs Howard was able to identify her husband's handwriting.

In the Hands of Savages

Found November 1877
On the shore at Luce Bay, Wigtownshire

In a bottle, written in pencil on a piece of paper, the writing very much faded:

On the 29th April, 1876, the ship Herclades was wrecked on the extremity of Patagonia. Crew in the hands of savages. Bring us assistance, my God. Latitude 24, longitude 21. [indistinct] Sighted a vessel.

Wigtownshire is in south west Scotland, more than 7,000 miles from the South American region of Patagonia.

Champagne Bottle

Found 25 June 1901
In the dockyard basin, Portsmouth

In a champagne bottle:

Steamship Tiger about to sink after colliding with a steam trawler off Cape Finisterre. Trawler and all hands lost. Captain and mate of Tiger drowned. We have committed ourselves to God. June 1st 1900, William Wright, second mate.

Cape Finisterre is at the western-most point of Spain. During Roman times it was considered to be the edge of the known world.

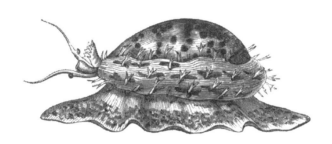

Cowrie

Murder and Suicide

Found 17 September 1889
Floating in Albert Quay, Belfast

In a bottle, on a slip of paper:

Look out for the body of a man in the Blackstaff who committed murder and suicide, and also for the murdered man. 6 p.m. 10/8/89.

The words "murder and suicide" were written in red ink, and the handwriting was said to be "stiff and cramped". The Blackstaff is an underground river in Belfast that was culverted and built over in the 1880s. The message was found by a man named Samuel McAfee, who passed it to the harbour police.

"Of course a hoax may be intended by some mischievous person," said the *Lancaster Gazette*, "but when taken into account that a body was seen floating in the lough about a fortnight ago, the strange find may possibly bear some significance."

Three Kisses

Found 8 March 1912
On the foreshore at Thorngumbald, near Hull

In a screw-stopper bottle, written in copying ink:

Good-bye, wife and children dear. x x x

Thomas Wiltshire.

23 Southcoates-lane, Hull, January 1st, 1912.

This message was found by James Gardner on the banks of the Humber Estuary near his home. The message was damp and the ink had smudged, making the address difficult to read. Mr Gardner's son made enquiries in Hull but could not trace the address.

Waiting Assistance

Found 26 June 1911
On the beach near Eyemouth, Berwickshire

In a black bottle:

October 20, 1910.

Gleaner waiting assistance from boat Pilgrim.

G. TODD.

The deep sea fishing boat *Gleaner* left Eyemouth for the fishing grounds with a crew of seven. It was last seen on 31 October by local boat the *Pilgrim* during a strong northwesterly gale around 15 miles off St Abb's Head. "It was as rough an experience as I have seen," said the *Pilgrim*'s Captain Aitchison, "and since I first went to sea 20 years ago I have never met so much wind and sea." The *Gleaner* did not follow the *Pilgrim* home, and was thought to have foundered in the gale with the loss of all hands.

The loss "placed a gloom" over the close-knit Eyemouth community. Retired fisherman James Paterson lost two sons, a grandson and a son-in-law on board the *Gleaner*. According to one report, it was Mr Paterson who found the message in a bottle, during his regular Sunday morning walk on the beach. The handwriting was confirmed by family members to belong to George Todd, who was married with children. The seven crewmembers left behind four widows and 16 children.

Oriole Torpedoed

Found 20 March 1915
Les Hanois, Guernsey

In a beer bottle, written on the front of a General Steam Navigation Company envelope:

Oriole torpedoed – sinking.

The merchant steamship *Oriole* left London on 29 January 1915 and was due to arrive in La Havre on the following day. On 6 February, two lifebuoys bearing the *Oriole*'s name were found near Rye, East Sussex. It was feared the ship had been sunk by a German submarine, which had previously torpedoed two other boats. "There is grave reason to fear that she may have fallen a victim to the German submarine which torpedoed the *Tokomaru* and the *Ilkaria*," said a Royal Navy statement. The *Oriole* had a crew of 21 hands. An expert compared the signatures of the crew, and it was determined that the message had been written by the ship's carpenter, Frank Swain.

All the Boys Merry

Found 5 November 1914
Brightstone, Isle of Wight

In a bottle, on two sides of a piece of paper:

Sunday, September 10th.

From some boys of the Warwicks off for the final at Berlin. Signed T.H. Rafferty, J.H. Scott, S. Rollins, S.W. Owen, T.C.L. Rosser, T. Hubball, and B. Rawlins.

All the boys merry under strenuous conditions. Hope the finder is O.K. Write to wife and baby.

Mrs Rafferty, 8, Hailliley Street, Handsworth.

The 1st Battalion of the Royal Warwickshire Regiment sailed from Southampton to Boulogne on board the SS *Caledonia* on 22 September 1914. Thomas Henry Rafferty, the writer of this message, was a tramway worker from Handsworth, Birmingham. He was married with a daughter. He was killed in action at Ypres on 25 April 1915. His body was never found.

The Rosalka is Aground

Found 10 October 1893
On the shore at Riga, Latvia

In a bottle:

The Rosalka is aground. Pray to God for our rescue.

FREELOFF

The *Rosalka* or *Rusalka* (*Water Nymph*) was a Russian monitor ship that sank during a storm in the Gulf of Finland on 7 September 1893 with the loss of 177 crew. The body of one crew member was found floating in a dinghy, along with several lifebuoys. The wreck of the *Rusalka* was eventually found in 2003, 110 years after it had sunk.

Sole Survivors

Found September 1903
On the beach at Fukave Island, Tonga

In a tightly-corked wine bottle:

Will the finder of this inform Messrs. Barkfoot & Co. of Port Said that their schooner, Ethel, foundered about 1,000 miles from Bombay? This note is written by the sole survivors, Capt. Lee and Seaman Thomas, who are in their last hopes.

Signed, J. T. Lee, Jan. 26 or 27, 1897.

The message was forwarded to the *New Zealand Herald* by a Captain Lombard of Tongatabu, and published without comment. Several months later, it was published in several US newspapers, with the added detail that the British schooner *Ethel* had disappeared while on route from Bombay to its home port of Port Said, Egypt. However, no reference to the *Ethel*, nor Barkfoot & Co, appeared in British newspapers.

Please Let My Dear Wife Know

Found 14 November 1897
On the beach at Dartmouth Harbour, Devon

In a white spirit bottle:

Going down now at Flamborough Head. S.S Princess of Sunderland, Nov 13 1893. Should any one pick this up please to let my dear wife know, lives at 25 Lawrence Street, Sunderland. Engines are broken down. God help us. Going down every minute. Good bye all, my wife and little ones. May God for give me all.

Signed, Mustard A.B.

Princes of Sunderland, Nov 13 1893

The Gale of 1893 was a violent storm that wrecked numerous vessels and took around 200 lives over the course of 48 hours around the British Isles. The *Princess* was returning to its home port of Sunderland from Bilbao with a cargo of iron ore. By the time it reached the North Sea, the storm had reached hurricane force. According to one report, "the sea was running mountains high, and the hurricane was accompanied by blinding showers."

The ship was spotted in distress by the coastguard at Flamborough Head, a chalk cliff promontory on the Yorkshire coast. The coastguard attempted to fire a safety line using the rocket apparatus life-saving device, but the ship drifted north onto rocks and was smashed to pieces. A piece of the ship bearing its name was washed up on the rocks. All 19 crew members died. Three smaller ships were wrecked on the same rocks during the storm.

The *Princess* was Sunderland-built and was owned by John Sanderson, the Mayor of Sunderland. All of the crew were from the Sunderland area. Robert Mustard was an able-bodied seaman (A.B.). The message was found, almost exactly four years to the day after the wreck and having drifted for more than 500 miles around the English coast, by Dartmouth bridge engineer George Humphrey. It was passed via Customs House authorities and the Board of Trade to Mustard's widow.

To the Bottom of the Sea

Found August 1900
Near Baker Beach, San Francisco, California

In a bottle:

Winfield Chevalier: I have ended my life by going to the bottom of the sea. All friends, farewell. Henry Beaumont.

The message was found by George Boke, who passed it to Police Chief Sullivan for investigation.

Limpet

Sources

Introduction, *Sheffield Evening Telegraph*, 16 January 1893, *Exeter and Plymouth Gazette*, 30 June 1899, *South Wales Daily News*, 1 July 1899, *Guardian*, 19 April 2016, *Chamber's Journal* quoted in *New York Times*, 24 October 1880, *London Standard* quoted in *Lincolnshire Chronicle*, 6 August 1897

Cold Ocean (*Naronic*), *Dundee Courier*, 16 July 1896

Look After My Boy (*City of Boston*), *Boston Advertiser*, 9 May 1871

Love From Hubert, *Lancashire Evening Post*, 10 January 1907

The Body in a Well, *Illustrated Police News* and *Canterbury Journal*, 10 October 1896

Inside A Cod (*Lucio*), *Sheffield Independent*, 15 February 1897

Forgive Me (*Yoular*), *Aberdeen Evening Express*, 3 June 1889

I Know I Cannot Escape (*Pacific*), *Bedfordshire Times* and *Shipping and Mercantile Gazette*, 30 July 1861

A Pretty Little Boy (*Beautiful Star*), *Huddersfield Chronicle*, 21 February 1873

Death Stares Us In, *New York Times*, 24 March 1892

Titanic Sinking (*Titanic*), *Chicago Day Book*, 31 July 1912, *Scotsman*, 12 October 1912, BBC News website, 26 October 2011

Torpedoed (*Membland*), *Dundee Evening Telegraph*, 25 November 1915

Drowned in Atlantic, *Dundee Courier*, 17 August 1914

Ready to Meet My God (*Lucie*), *Savannah Advertiser*, 10 November 1874, *New York Times*, 15 November 1874

Send Us Help or We Are Lost (*Atlanta*), *New York Times*, 7 August, 1883

Not a Soldier, *London Daily News*, 26, 29 May, 5, 6 June 1906

Sixteen Days Without Water, *New Zealand Herald*, 20 March 1896

Lost Three Men Overboard (*Cape of Good Hope*), *New York Times*, 29 July 1883

I Expect My Turn Will Come Next (*Bavaria*), *New York Times*, 18 June 1889

Don't Expect To Get Ashore (*Hattie Fisher*), *New York Times*, 7 September 1885

Have Sprung a Leak (*Vedette*), *New York Times*, 13 December 1896

If Anything Happens (*Waratah*), *Manchester Courier*, 13 January 1914, *Auckland Star*, 28 February 1914

Please Send This to My Aunt (*Margaret*), *New York Times*, 7 August 1881

Miss Charlesworth's Compliments, *Exeter and Plymouth Gazette*, 13 January 1909

Trois Freres, *New York Times*, 2 August 1874

Rewarded For Their Kindness (*Julia*), *New York Times*, 10 November 1895

Farewell Forever, *New York Times*, 22 January 1888

All Well (*Erebus* and *Terror*), *New York Times* and *San Francisco Chronicle*, 17 September 1869

100 Horses (*Lady Anne*), *Aberdeen Evening Express*, 28 August 1889

Spanish Steamer Opened Fire (*Enore*), *Cardiff Evening Express*, 1 July 1898

Run Over by a Steamer (*Borregaard*), *Nottingham Evening Post*, 30 July 1904

The Sea Is Offal Heavy (*Prince Wales*), *Exeter and Plymouth Gazette*, 15 October 1892

Lifting of the Body, *Dundee Evening Telegraph*, 12 February 1883

May the Lord Comfort My Mother (*Caller Ou*), *Sheffield Evening Telegraph*, 16 January 1893

Mutiny (*Angus*), *Aberdeen Journal*, 11 July 1914

Know I Died Happy (*Spanish Queen*), *Times*, 18 September 1866

Laden with Paraffin (*Diana*), *Inverness Courier*, 27 June 1867

Dying Blessing (*County of Carnarvon*), *Newcastle Morning Herald*, 7 January 1890

Thirteen Shipwrecked Refugees (*Tamaris*), *Pall Mall Gazette*, 9 May 1888

Drifting for Hours, *New York Sun*, 15 August 1891

Leaking Badly (*Smuggler*), *New York Times*, 24, 25 July 1883

A Fearful Day (*Mary Hopp*), *Shields Daily Gazette*, 8 April 1889

Everything Is Destroyed (*Bay*), *Dundee Courier*, 25 December 1876, *Freeman's Journal*, 1 March 1877, *Liverpool Mercury*, 3 March 1877

Detained on Island, *Evening Times-Republican*, 23 April, 1906, *Rock Island Argus*, 27 April 1906

Kept There by Force, *Daily Eagle*, 29 July 1901

Gone Down in the Bay of Biscay (*Hiero*), *Dundee Courier*, 21 August 1861

A Cargo of Cotton (*City of New York*), *Shields Daily Gazette*, 1 September 1866

Cannot Get Away (*Peti Dubrovacki*), *Buckingham Advertiser*, 17 February 1877

Washed Away During Gale (*Sarah Jane*), *Aberdare Times*, 5 October 1895

We Are In Great Distress (*Juno*), *Dublin Evening Packet*, 8 March 1861

A Harbour I Will Never See (*Caledonia*), *Belfast News-Letter*, 27 February 1865, *Londonderry Standard*, 17 February 1866

Nora Will Get Over It in Time, *Times*, 3 June 1867

The Secret of Her Birth, *Belfast News-Letter*, 4 February 1869, *Lincolnshire Chronicle*, 19 February 1869

Seen Whale, *Aberdeen Express*, 4 September 1894

Fearful Hurricane (*Atalanta*), *Liverpool Mercury*, 29
    April 1880, *London Evening Standard*, 26 April 1880,
    Portsmouth Evening News, 8 May 1880

Clinging to the Mast (*Elsie*), *Hartlepool Mail*, 16
    March 1897

No More Whisky, *Straits Times*, 18 September 1912

Shipwrecked on Sandbank (*Annaberga*), *Sheffield
    Independent* and *Sheffield Daily Telegraph*, 4
    February 1878

In Frail Boats (*Pelican*), *San Francisco Call*, 31 May
    1899, 11 September 1901

Six Inches Per Hour (*Mary Ann*), *Dundee Evening
    Telegraph*, 18 June 1879

To The Foaming Deep (*Horatia*), *Times*, 9 January
    1861

Living on Raw Penguins (*Firefly*), *New Zealand Press*,
    26 November 1878

Looking Out For a Sail (*Lilian*), *Morning Advertiser*, 2
    September 1871

Crew on Half Whack (*Samoena*), *Lancashire Evening
    Post*, 8 May 1900

Good Soil (*Zoe*), *London Standard* quoted in
    Lincolnshire Chronicle, 6 August 1897

Too Heavily Laden (*London*), *Era*, 4 March 1866,
    Reynold's Newspaper, 25 March 1866, *Newcastle
    Journal*, 13 September 1867

Down to Plimsoll's Mark (*Wells*), *Shields Gazette* 4
January 1877, *Middlesbrough Gazette* 24 February
1877

In Sight of Land, *Edinburgh News*, 3 February 1894

Lost Off Lundy (*Isabel*), *Western Mail*, 10 May 1875

A Sober, Industrious Young Man, *Washington Times*,
23 March, 1897

Condition Sink (*Amelia*), *Edinburgh Evening News*, 15
October 1892

Sea Messenger (*Cambria*), *Chelsea News and General
Advertiser*, 3 December 1870

1702 (*Clown*), *Yorkshire Post*, 7 June 1903

Norwegian at Sea, *Sheffield Evening Telegraph*, 6
September 1893

The Walrus is Sinking (*Walrus*), *Scotsman*, 28, 29
June 1911

A Token of My Respect (*Shima Maru*), *Melbourne
Argus*, 9 July 1914, *Grey River Argus*, 23 July 1914

I Was Shot Last Night (*WC Cook*), *Ravalli Republican*,
28 April 1897

Bear Hotel (*Canada*), *Staffs Sentinel*, 21 March 1912

Highland Lassie, *Hull Daily Mail*, 12 July 1905

Dreadfull Weather (*Marie Stuart*), *Liverpool Mercury*,
3 April 1883

Turned Over Sunday Night (*Huronian*), *Dundee
Evening Post*, 21 March, 27 June 1902, *Nottingham
Evening Post*, 2 January 1907

All Hands Will Perish (*Mary Jane*), *Sunderland Echo* and *Shields Gazette*, 18 February 1879, *Berwickshire News and General Advertiser*, 25 February 1879

Remains of the Dundee Whaler (*Snowdrop*), *Scotsman*, 11 March, 17, 20, 27 September, 4, 18 October 1909, *Dundee Courier* 5 October 1910

If Our Remains Be Found (*Firefly*), *Times*, 19 September 1889

God Help Us (*Lizzie*), *Glasgow Herald*, 9 December 1898

Steamer Combat (*Combat*), *Yorkshire Post*, 30 July 1875

Consigned to the Thames, *South Bucks Standard*, 5 May 1905

Ship Ariosto (*Ariosto*), *Preston Chronicle*, 21 June 1890

New York Stock Exchange (*Nancy*), *South Wales Daily News*, 17 February 1900

Going to My Doom (*Nutfield*), *Western Times*, 4 March 1913

In the Hands of Savages (*Hercaldes*), *Edinburgh Evening News*, 3 November 1877

Champagne Bottle (*Tiger*), *Portsmouth Evening News*, 25 June 1901

Murder and Suicide (*Blackstaff*), *Belfast News-Letter*, 18 September 1889, *Lancaster Gazette*, 21 September 1889

Three Kisses, *Hull Daily Mail*, 12 March 1912

Waiting Assistance (*Gleaner*), *Berwick Advertiser*, 30
  June 1911, *Aberdeen Journal*, 3 November 1910,
  Berwickshire News, 8 November 1910
Oriole Torpedoed (*Oriole*), *Birmingham Daily Post*, 31
  July 1915
All the Boys Merry (*Caledonia*), *Birmingham Mail*, 21
  November 1914
The Rosalka is Aground (*Rosalka*), *Los Angeles Herald*,
  11 October 1893
Sole Survivors (*Ethel*), *New Zealand Herald*, 28
  September 1903, *San Juan County Index*, 11 March
  1904
Please Let My Dear Wife Know (*Princess*), *Sunderland
  Echo*, 20 November 1893, *Shields Gazette*, 16
  December 1897
To the Bottom of the Sea, *San Francisco Call*, 8
  August 1900
Endpaper messages: (*Rechta*) *Middlesbrough Gazette*,
  26 May 1899, (*Britannia*) *Suffolk and Essex Free
  Press*, 4 August 1886, (*Island King*) *Sheffield Evening
  Telegraph*, 6 October 1902, (*Louisa*) *Shields Gazette*,
  14 February 1881, (*S Vaughn*) *Edinburgh Evening
  News*, 28 October 1881, (*Stella*) *Hartlepool Mail*, 30
  June 1899

Cod

MESSAGES FROM THE SEA.

From Dunkirk it is stated that a workman passing on the beach at Rosendael, noticed a small bundle of letters floating close to the shore. Entering the water, he picked them up, and found that they were attached to a block of wood. As they were written in English, he took them to the British Consulate. These letters were stamped and ready for posting; and, although soaked with water, the addresses were quite legible. One was open, the envelope having given way. It was dated April 4, and written from the Kentish Knock Light-vessel. No fear of shipwreck is entertained. It is supposed that the crew of the Kentish Knock Light-vessel, wishing to have their letters posted, attempted to throw them to some homeward-bound ship, and that the parcel accidentally fell overboard. The letters, which have been forwarded to England, have been afloat fourteen or fifteen days, and have, nevertheless, come to land with stamps and contents intact. The fact of their having been picked up at Rosendael, while thrown overboard from the Kentish Knock, constitutes a valuable hint to navigators as to the direction of the currents.

A MESSAGE FROM THE SEA.

Yesterday morning a coffee canister, to which was fastened a piece of cork, was found by a boy on the beach near Ilfracombe. It contained the following note: "To my wife and children.—The Stella is going down as I pen my last words. If I do not survive go to my brother. Good-bye, my loved ones, Good-bye.—R. Neel, A.B., to Mrs Abigail Neel, 5, High-street, Cardiff." The note was written in pencil on a piece of paper torn from a diary.

READ MORE:

MESSAGES FROM THE SEA is a website collecting fascinating messages from a lost era found washed up in bottles on shores around the world:

www.messagesfromthesea.com
Twitter: @messagesfromsea

PAUL BROWN is a writer living on the north-east coast of England and specialising in extraordinary true stories and also the strange history of football:

www.stuffbypaulbrown.com
Twitter: @paulbrownUK

ALSO AVAILABLE by the same author:

SINS DYED IN BLOOD
The Lost Pirate of Blackbeard's Golden Age
Edward Robinson was a British pirate who sailed with Blackbeard during the Golden Age of Piracy in the early 1700s. But was he really a murderous sea-robber, and did he deserve his brutal fate? This is the true swashbuckling story of a forgotten pirate.

eBook available from Amazon and iTunes

FROM A BLOOD-RED SEA
The Last Voyage of Daniel Collins
Winter, 1824. Merchant seaman Daniel Collins is shipwrecked in shark-infested waters a hundred miles from land, then brutally attacked by a gang of pirates. His crewmates are murdered, but Collins escapes, and begins an epic journey across land and sea in a desperate effort to reach civilisation, and to find a way home. For fans of *The Revenant* and *In the Heart of the Sea*, this forgotten true story is one of the most remarkable tales of survival ever told.

eBook available from Amazon and iTunes

THE ROCKETBELT CAPER
A True Tale of Invention, Obsession and Murder
When three men set out on a quest to build a Buck Rogers-style flying machine, their obsession with the Rocketbelt 2000 shatters their friendship and sets in motion a chain of events involving theft, kidnapping, and murder. From sci-fi to reality, this is the entirely true story of the amazing rocketbelt.

Paperback available from good bookshops
eBook available from Amazon and iTunes

www.superelasticbooks.com

25755321R00118

Printed in Great Britain
by Amazon